WALKING
IN THE
SPIRIT

Studies in the Fruit of the Spirit

Zenas J. Bicket

GOSPEL PUBLISHING HOUSE
SPRINGFIELD, MISSOURI
02-0611

WALKING IN THE SPIRIT

Printed in the United States of America
Library of Congress Catalog Card Number 76-51000
International Standard Book Number 0-88243-611-2

Contents

I
You Must Bear Fruit

THESE ARE EXCITING DAYS in the body of Christ. As never before since the first century, the Spirit of God is moving. All nations and all peoples are feeling the refreshing breath of the Holy Spirit. His supernatural move among the most unlikely people is demonstrating that the body of Christ includes many more than we at one time thought.

This unprecedented move of the Spirit, certainly a reminder that we are living in the end times, has been accompanied by signs and wonders. Man recognizes the presence of God, for the demonstration and power of the Spirit confirm the truth of God's Word. Signs bring great edification and blessing to those who come in obedience to the God who is pressing His claims so eloquently through the mighty flow of the Spirit. The Church is being revived, its members are being identified, and men and women everywhere are coming to know Christ as the Saviour of their souls.

This is the exciting aspect of the growth of God's kingdom on earth. Like the multitudes who flocked to see the miracles of Jesus, we want to be where the action is. Groups of Christians gather to study the gifts and ministries of the Spirit, seeking for their own lives the miraculous manifestations and ministries. This desire should not be discouraged. But it must be balanced by the teaching and study of what Spirit-filled Christians are called by God to be. Too many are more concerned about what God wants them *to do* than about what He wants them *to be*. Jesus calls every Christian to spiritual perfection—to become a person of a divine nature rather than a carnal or worldly nature.

The Fruit—Marks of Spirituality

What exactly does God want His children to be? What are the marks of character to be found in the Christian who pleases God? What sets him apart from the world and from the majority of professing Christians who sit comfortably in the pew each Sunday morning? The marks of spirituality, contrary to what many people think, are not the *gifts* of the Spirit, but the *fruit* of the Spirit.

We may sincerely feel that supernatural gifts and manifestations prove the spirituality of a person. A single miracle frequently authenticates everything the miracle worker does or speaks. But God's Word unmistakably warns us not to fall into this error:

Though I speak with the tongues of men and of angels, . . . though I have the gift of prophecy, and understand all mysteries, and all knowledge; and though I have all faith, so that I could remove mountains, and have not charity [love], I am nothing (1 Corinthians 13:1,2).

A miracle worker may be nothing in God's sight, but the one who manifests divine love is pleasing to God. Character is more important than miracles.

Jesus said it just as forcefully as Paul did:

Ye shall know them by their fruits. . . . Every good tree bringeth forth good fruit; but a corrupt tree bringeth forth evil fruit. A good tree cannot bring forth evil fruit, neither can a corrupt tree bring forth good fruit. Every tree that bringeth not forth good fruit is hewn down, and cast into the fire. Wherefore by their fruits ye shall know them (Matthew 7:16-20).

Fruit bearing is not as spectacular as demonstrating the gifts, but it is more important in determining spirituality. In the same passage Jesus continues:

Many will say to me in that day, Lord, Lord, have we not prophesied in thy name? and in thy name have cast out devils? and in thy name done many wonderful works? And then will I profess unto them, I never knew you: depart from me, ye that work iniquity (vv. 22,23).

The fruit of the Spirit (the marks of spirituality or the character traits that are pleasing to God) are love, joy, peace, patience, kindness, goodness, faith or faithfulness, meekness, and self-control. The Christian who lacks even one of these fruit has a defect in his character, while the lack of a specific gift has no such meaning. "Have all the gifts of healing? do all speak with tongues? do all interpret?" (1 Corinthians 12:30). The answer is no. A missing gift has no such meaning.

"Have all the gifts of healing? do all speak with tongues? do all interpret?" (1 Corinthians 12:30). The answer is no. A missing gift in a single life is not a sign of spiritual deficiency. Nor is spirituality measured by the number or frequency with which the gifts operate. But if any of the fruit are missing, God's ideal for our lives has not been achieved.

Producing the True Fruit

How can we recognize the fruit of the Spirit in the life of a Christian? Are not love, joy, peace, patience, kindness, goodness, faithfulness, meekness, and self-control to be found in people who do not even profess to be Christians, to say nothing about being filled with the Spirit? But the fruit of the Spirit are not ordinary virtues or character traits. They cannot be manufactured or counterfeited by human effort. They are supernatural qualities that only the Spirit can produce.

There is a love to be found in the world; human love might even be willing to die for a child, a parent, or a friend. But divine love is willing to die for an enemy, and the fruit of the Spirit is divine love dwelling in a human life. The world can know happiness and joy—when things are going well. But the joy of the Lord is produced by the Spirit even in tribulation and suffering. The world has peace when conflict and war are suppressed. But the supernatural peace, of God is confidence and serenity in the midst of natural pressures and conflicts.

Through the work of the Spirit, the Christian can be patient with people and circumstances, kind to the unkind, consistently good and benevolent, faithful in the midst of disappointment and suffering, meek even when mistreated by those against whom retaliation would produce some justice, and self-controlled in the presence of bounty and blessing. The same virtues in the world are limited and incomplete. Man can be patient, kind, faithful, and meek in his dealings with those he loves and respects. But he cannot in his own strength demonstrate those virtues toward his enemies or toward those who make no effort to reciprocate the goodwill.

The Fruit in the Life of Jesus

If the fruit of the Spirit are supernatural character traits rather than human virtues, where can we look to see a pattern for the fruit in our lives? To look at others, even at sincere and devoted Christians, will not suffice. There will be points at which the example will fall short. Instead we must look at a divine example for the perfect pattern of these supernatural virtues. Each one of the nine fruit can be seen in the life of Jesus. Throughout the Gospels shine the love of God, the joy of the Lord, the peace of Christ, the patience and kindness of God, the goodness of the Lord, the faithfulness of God, and the meekness and self-control of Christ—all through the person of the Son of God. One of the most rewarding studies of Scripture is to read the life of Christ looking for manifestations of the fruit of the Spirit. They can be found in concentrated frequency in the story of Christ's passion (John 13-21).

Not only is Jesus the pattern and example for a life of fruit bearing, He is the source of the fruit. "As the branch cannot bear fruit of itself, except it abide in the vine; no more can ye, except ye abide in me" (15:4). Fruit bearing also has some pain, even for the branch that abides in the True Vine. "Every branch that beareth fruit, he purgeth it, that it may bring forth more fruit" (v. 2). Yet it is the vine into which the branch is grafted that determines the fruit that is produced. A branch that abides in a natural or carnal vine cannot bring forth the good fruit of the Spirit. But when we are grafted into Christ, the Holy Spirit causes the fruit-bearing life of Christ to flow through us. Without the vine, the branch can do nothing (v. 5).

Bringing Glory to the Father

Too many Christians are careless or unconcerned about the presence of the fruit in their lives. They live and speak as though the fruit of the Spirit are a little frosting on the cake of Christian experience. But the cake is still a cake without the frosting.

Not so with the fruit of the Spirit! The nine fruit are the essential ingredients in the Christian life that pleases God. Nor can one leave the option of producing fruit to the omnipotence of God. The attitude among many seems to be, "If God wants to produce the fruit in me, I'm available." Such a response is actually a hindrance to the work of the Spirit. We must be so desirous of demonstrating the fruit of the Spirit that we remove any hindrance of unconcern, carelessness, or disobedience so the life of Christ can flow through us to produce the marks of spiritual character.

The fruit of the Spirit are not for personal edification only. The lack of the fruit brings shame and reproach on Christianity. Their presence in a life brings glory to God. "Herein is my Father glorified, that ye bear much fruit; so shall ye be my disciples" (John 15:8). Again, the mark of spirituality, the evidence of a life that brings glory to God, is the presence of the fruit of the Spirit.

As you begin your study of the individual fruit of the Spirit throughout the following chapters, make the prayer of Paul in Colossians 1:9-11 the theme of your prayerful study:

We ask God that you may receive from him all wisdom and spiritual understanding for full insight into his will, so that your manner of life may be worthy of the Lord and entirely pleasing to him. We pray that you may bear fruit in active goodness of every kind, and grow in the knowledge of God. May he strengthen you, in his glorious might, with ample power to meet whatever comes with fortitude, patience, and joy (*NEB*).

proclaiming the absence of love in the world home

II
Love and the Spirit-filled Life

LOVE IS ONE OF THE MOST MISUNDERSTOOD of the Christian virtues. The whole of society, including the contemporary church, shows its misunderstanding of this foremost trait in either God or man by loudly proclaiming the absence of love in the world. Some fragment its meaning. For them, love is the missing element that keeps others from sharing possessions and gains with the have-nots. Their counterparts in the Establishment distrust such demands in the name of love and so exclude the "love-mongers" from church and community.

Others have so diluted the concept of love that it is mere sentimentality. If hate is not our motivation, they reason, then we certainly possess love. To them, love is a warm feeling—whether toward another person, a mistreated French poodle, or even a misused environment. From the ease of the TV chair they feel for, or "love," the starving of India, the suffering family of an assassinated political figure, or the victims of a tragic mine disaster.

Still others have bent the idea of love so it is hardly recognizable. Love is license, freedom to allow the baser passions to roam undisciplined over the whole area of human experience. If one feels attracted to a partner, the stirring is love and justifies the greatest intimacy, regardless of community codes and mores. In fact, these restrictions are seen as the great enemies of this misshapen concept of love.

Some who hold to this concept, unwilling to be classed as complete libertines, bring man's fallen reason before God's court of judgment, hoping to satisfy themselves that whatever is, is right. This new morality appeals to love for its justification. If love is better served by compromising the ethical standards and religious teachings of the community, then moral law may be violated according to love's need. But situation ethics is simply an accommodation to contemporary culture.

Such a misunderstanding and abuse of love is no recent phenomenon. Jonathan Edwards, in the midst of America's Great Awakening of the 18th century, recognized that all that stirred in the heart of natural man was not divine love:

This may be from some extraordinary powerful influence of Satan and some great delusion; but [it] is nothing but nature extraordinarily acted. . . . It is of great importance and use . . . to discover and demonstrate the delusions of Satan, in many kinds of false religious affections, which multitudes are deluded by, and probably have been in all ages of the Christian church.[1]

Love, then, is neither wrong action rationalized by a bent definition of love nor a passive emotion which warms the rib cage. It is, instead, a deliberate act of the will, motivated by the welfare of the recipient, for true love must have an external object. John, the apostle of love, understood the active nature of love:

---

[1] Jonathan Edwards, *Religious Affections,* ed., John E. Smith (New Haven: Yale University Press, 1959), pp. 209, 210.

"My little children, let us not love in word, neither in tongue; but in deed and in truth" (1 John 3:18).

Love—the Essence of God

The starting point of any investigation of love and the Spirit-filled life is, of necessity, 1 John 4:16. "God is love; and he that dwelleth in love dwelleth in God, and God in him." Some critics, overlooking the single purpose of all Sacred Writ, limit the love aspect of God to the New Testament, choosing rather to see a God of judgment in the Old Testament. But such interpretation misses the fundamental truth of God's nature. Without attempting to define God's love, Deuteronomy 7:7,8 simply states: "The Lord did not set his love upon you, nor choose you, because ye were more in number than any people; . . . but because the Lord loved you." Yet skeptics see only judgment in the God of the Old Testament.

It was the first night after the funeral of the mother of a young family. Both father and daughter were feeling the empty void of the quiet, darkened house. After long hours of wakefulness for both, little Susan called out from her bedroom, "Daddy, you love through the dark, don't you?"

The great Gift of Love, by whom we today "perceive . . . the love of God, because he laid down his life for us" (1 John 3:16), had not yet come in the full light of grace. Yet the God of the Old Testament loved through the dark.

Unfortunately, though the evidence of God's love, in the person and work of His Son Jesus Christ, has been once and for all revealed to the world, both sinners and Christians today fail to recognize that love. Christian parents tell their misbehaving children, "God is always watching you, and when you do wrong, He sees and remembers." How much more faithful to the Word would be, "God loves you so much He cannot take His eyes off you."

The love of God is an ocean; no line can sound its depths. It is a continent of unexplored expanse; no survey can find its boundary. It is a universe of infinity; no Apollo can reach its height. It is a mine of wealth; no delving can exhaust its riches. We may speak—we may sing—of the love of God, but until it is so vital that we naturally reflect its brilliance to God himself and to others, we have not comprehended it.

Love—the Mirror of God's Love

More frequent in Scripture than reference to God's love for man is the command that man should love God. To love God, the Old Testament implies, is to find pleasure in Him and strive diligently after Him, to seek Him for His own sake. Throughout the Old Testament, love is a definite act of the will, not an impulse which overwhelms man.

It is at this point that Paul and his New Testament contemporaries had to select with care the specific Greek word which would carry this meaning. The Greek word *eros* would not, for it denoted a general love of the world, seeking pleasure and satisfaction for the self. It motivated a person through impulse and intoxication. It mastered man by leaving him no choice, will, or freedom. The New Testament writers found no occasion to include this type of love in Holy Scripture. On a score of occasions, though, New Testament writers found *philos*, love for friends, to carry the weight of meaning.

For the majority of uses, however, neither of these two common Greek words would suffice. The lesser-known *agape,* with its ability to describe love as decisive action, not impulsive intoxication, was pressed into service and thereby became the great theological word for all succeeding generations.

Jesus himself taught the full meaning of all-absorbing love—love of God with a passionate devotion:

> To love God is to exist for Him as a slave for his lord (cf. Luke 17:7ff.). It is to listen faithfully and obediently to His orders, to place oneself under His lordship, to value above all else the realization of this lordship (cf. Matthew 6:33). It also means, however, to base one's whole being on God, to cling to Him with unreserved confidence, to leave with Him all care or final responsibility, to live by His hand. It is to hate and despise all that does not serve God nor come from Him, to break with all other ties, to cut away all that hinders (Matthew 5:29f.), to snap all bonds except that which binds to God alone.[2]

What in the world can prompt such a love in a human heart and will? Nothing! It demands impulse from the world of love—from God. As John says, we love Him only because He first loved us (1 John 4:19). Love is that bond of perfectness (Colossians 3:14) which eternally links frail man with Almighty Power.

Fear is a natural human trait; it is the sign of frailty. But there is no fear in love, for "perfect love casteth out fear" (1 John 4:18). Only God's love is perfect, but as man mirrors that love to his Heavenly Father, fear vanishes. In His will we need fear nothing, for He loves us with a perfect love.

Mirrored love is obedient love. "This is love, that we walk after his commandments" (2 John 6). The

---

[2] Ethelbert Stauffer, *Theological Dictionary of the New Testament*, ed., Gerhard Kittel (Grand Rapids: Wm. B. Eerdmans Publishing Co., 1964), I, 45.

usual rendering of 1 John 5:2, "By this we know that we love the children of God, when we love God, and keep his commandments," can just as well be translated, ". . . when we love God, that is, keep His commandments." But mirrored love is not merely obedience; it is *loving* obedience. What we once felt we had to do, mirrored love makes us want to do.

Love—the Royal Law

Love is the essence of God. And it is our loving response to a God of love. Finally, it is the basis for all wholesome human relationships. "If ye fulfill the royal law according to the Scripture, Thou shalt love thy neighbor as thyself, ye do well" (James 2:8). This is not a principle which we hold up to others to encourage favorable treatment. It is for me in my contacts with you and other neighbors. It is for you in situations where you touch other neighbors. On this matter, we are individually accountable to no one but God himself, yet herein is our love measured.

The concept of loving one's neighbor goes back to the Old Testament, Jesus simply reaffirmed it. But Jesus went one step further than Jewish tradition when He demanded that His followers love their enemies. Such a command practically anticipates the outpouring of the Holy Spirit on the Day of Pentecost.

Love God? Yes. Love neighbors? Yes. Both of these commands can be understood and, if not fulfilled perfectly, at least given full agreement by diligent human effort. But to love one's enemies! That demands a measure of Spirit endowment far beyond all logic and reason. In the power of the same Spirit available to us today, Jesus said, "Father, forgive them; for they know not what they do" (Luke 23:34).

> *Love ever gives—*
> *Forgives—outlives*
> *And ever stands*
> *With open hands.*
> *And while it lives—*
> *It gives.*
> *For this is love's prerogative*
> *To give, and give, and give.*
> *—Oxenham*

Cannot giving, the mark of love, be counterfeited? Do not unbelievers exhibit love, often more consistently than church members? There is a natural love that partakes of some of the characteristics of divine love; but the natural, no matter how noble, must never be allowed to substitute for the divine.

Both spiritual love and natural ... cause desires after the object beloved; but they be not the same sort of desires; there is a sensation of soul in the spiritual desires of one that loves God, which is entirely different from all natural desires: . . . Natural men have conceptions of many things about spiritual affections; but there is something in them which . . . they have no more conceptions of, than one born blind has of colors.[3]

There is a love which reaches beyond the natural affection; and there is a measure of love, even in the life of a Christian, which is the consistent fruit of a Spirit-filled life. Paul speaks to the Colossians of their "love *in the Spirit*" (1:8). *Christian* love or *spiritual* love would have distinguished it from natural love, but Paul was thinking of that special measure of love which results from complete yieldedness to the Holy Spirit.

---

[3] Edwards, *op. cit.*, p. 208.

19

The great love chapter, 1 Corinthians 13, is sometimes seen as a contrast to chapters 12 and 14, a more excellent way which makes the operation of the gifts of the Spirit almost to be avoided. But its very placement between the charismatic chapters emphasizes the charismatic nature of this love. This love is patient and kind. It does not envy or grow proud—ever. It never behaves inappropriately, nor considers its own interests. It thinks only righteous thoughts. It never fails and will never pass away.

This is charismatic love—love which is not subject to the interruptions of human frailty as long as the believer remains Spirit-filled and yielded to the inner working of God's Holy Spirit. "The love of God is shed abroad in our hearts by the Holy Ghost" (Romans 5:5).

Of all the fruit of the Spirit mentioned by Paul in Galatians 5:22,23, the first is love.

The "love" which the Spirit produces in us is "the fruit" of Christ's life, and of His own life; not something different from it, which He can bestow upon us as a gift, but something of His own which springs up in us, because He is living within. This shows us that the first, the chief, the most notable thing in the Holy Ghost, when He dwells in us, is His love.[4]

Not only is love the first of a list of nine fruit, but it seems also to be a comprehensive term which includes all the eight which follow. It is almost as though Paul, using parallel ideas from his love chapter to the Corinthians, says that the fruit of the Spirit is charismatic love and then adds a definition of that

---

[4] James Elder Cumming, *Through the Eternal Spirit* (Minneapolis: Bethany Fellowship, Inc., 1965), pp. 127, 128.

love: that is, joy, peace, long-suffering, gentleness, goodness, faith, meekness, and temperance.

Joy is charismatic love in the midst of grief or sorrow—love rejoices in the truth. Peace is the love of God operating on conflict and turmoil—love is not easily provoked. Patience is the love of God in trial and testing—love beareth all things. Gentleness is the love of God in the voice of authority and of power— love vaunts not itself. Goodness or benevolence is God's love toward the less fortunate—love is kind. Faith acquires living force to the extent that it is active in love—love believes all of God's promises. Meekness is the knowledge of God's love in the moment of personal achievement or fame—love is not puffed up. Self-control is God's love in the presence of natural bounty and temporal blessing—love does not behave unseemly.

This is charismatic love, the fruit of a Spirit-filled life. Such love is supreme. It dares and does the impossible. It will still remain firm when the last selfish act, the last cruel ambition, the last deed of hate has been known. This love is the mainspring of the world, that which makes its object sweet or fair. Love lies at the root of all nobility, goodness, or heroism. The whole of God's dealing with wayward man, through the ages and yet today, is truly one great Love Story.

Love, charismatic love, is the most excellent way. And yet men persist in going other ways, to their own frustration and destruction. They choose rather the way led by the spirit of fear, Satan's counterfeit for God's Spirit of love. But the Spirit-filled life brings the remedy for fear: "God hath not given us the spirit of fear; but [He has given us the Spirit] of power, and of love . . ." (2 Timothy 1:7). It is our task merely to yield to and reflect that love.

21

III

Joy
and the
Spirit-filled Life

SHOULD A CHRISTIAN ALWAYS HAVE A SMILE on his face? Was Jesus a man of outward joy? Did He laugh with the disciples as they walked along Galilean roads?

Somehow, we find it difficult to think of Jesus as a man of happiness. He wept over Jerusalem because its inhabitants had rejected the peace He brought to them. He wept with Mary after Lazarus had been placed in the tomb, even though He must have known that the dead man would be raised to life. Jesus was hurt by the unbelief of the Jews to whom He ministered. He was grieved at the sin that held men and women in its bondage.

It is difficult to imagine a smiling Jesus in these circumstances. Yet He possessed a joy that He wants every Christian to experience. "These things have I spoken unto you, that my joy might remain in you, and that your joy might be full" (John 15:11). The world is under the blight of sin. It is filled with pain and hardship. These things make sad the heart of God, and Christians who share the sorrows of others likewise feel the sadness.

But the joy of the Lord, the second fruit of the Spirit, has little to do with light and carefree laughter or human happiness. In fact, the true fruit of joy is best seen against the backdrop of sorrow and suffering. This does not mean that the Christian never smiles; it simply means that the supernatural joy of the Holy Spirit is measured by inward confidence and optimism rather than by outward expression.

The Command to Be Joyful

There are no qualifications to the scriptural commands concerning joy. Paul said: "Rejoice in the Lord always." And just in case we do not catch the significance of the word *always*, Paul added, "and again I say, Rejoice" (Philippians 4:4). That means in sorrow and disappointment as well as when things are going smoothly. Peter also recognized that the joy of the Lord is different from the joy of the world. "Rejoice with joy unspeakable and full of glory" (1 Peter 1:8). Nothing is more unspeakable or indescribable than the God-given joy a Spirit-filled Christian can feel in the midst of trouble.

The early Christians demonstrated the joy of the Lord in the face of tribulation and testing. Paul commended the Thessalonians for enduring affliction and at the same time manifesting the joy of the Holy Spirit (1 Thessalonians 1:6). To the Colossians he said: "[I] rejoice in my sufferings for you" (Colossians 1:24). Only through the help of the Holy Spirit can a Christian actually thank those who are bringing pain into his life.

Very few Christians in the western world have had to endure suffering like the early Christians who stood for Christ in a pagan society. Becoming a Christian then meant loss of employment or livelihood. It sometimes meant loss of property to the state. More frequently it meant persecution from neighbors opposed to those who defected from the heathen traditions. Outbursts of anger and wrath against the Christians even resulted in destruction of property and possessions. How did the Early Church react to this persecution? The writer of Hebrews testified: "[You] took joyfully the spoiling of your goods, knowing in yourselves that ye have in heaven a better and an enduring substance." It was a special work of the Holy Spirit to impart the abiding joy of the Lord even while the Christians stood by and saw their possessions destroyed.

The early Christians also came into conflict with the magistrates and officials in the cities of Asia Minor and Europe. Not because they were criminals or law breakers, but because the oppenents of the gospel used every means possible to stifle the message of salvation. The disciples were beaten and imprisoned. They were brought before councils and juries, commanded not to mention the name of Jesus, and ordered to leave the area. But even as they left the presence of the magistrates, having suffered abuse and humiliation, they departed "rejoicing that they were counted worthy to suffer shame for his name" (Acts 5:41). The joy of the Lord is given by the Holy Spirit for any situation.

The Source of This Joy

What is the relationship between suffering and supernatural joy? Is suffering really necessary to demonstrate that one's joy is that which is produced supernaturally by the Holy Spirit? The answer to these questions is found in the last words Jesus shared with His disciples before going to the cross. "You have sorrow now, because I have said that I am going away," He told them. "But I will send you

25

a Comforter." Then Jesus summed up the relationship between suffering and joy in verses 20-22 of John 16. All three verses speak of sorrow and joy; they must be studied closely as a single unit.

Verily, verily, I say unto you, That ye shall weep and lament, but the world shall rejoice; and ye shall be sorrowful, but your sorrow shall be turned into joy (v. 20).

How is that sorrow turned into joy?

A woman when she is in travail hath sorrow, because her hour is come: but as soon as she is delivered of the child, she remembereth no more the anguish, for joy that a man is born into the world (v. 21).

Supernatural joy can exist in the midst of suffering because we know that something good will come out of the suffering. The suffering is seen as the birth pains of something special. Jesus then concluded His instruction on the source and permanence of joy.

And ye now therefore have sorrow: but I will see you again, and your heart shall rejoice, and your joy no man taketh from you (v. 22).

This imagery of travail and the joy of birth is seen throughout Scripture. The whole sinful creation groans and travails in pain (Romans 8:22), but out of the present pain of nature will come a new heaven and a new earth. Paul called the Galatians his "little children, of whom I travail in birth again until Christ be formed in you" (Galatians 4:19).

Paul had many experiences in which he could take delight. He spoke in tongues more than all the Corinthians. He had been the instrument through which God raised Eutychus from the dead (Acts 20:9). He had seen Jesus on the road to Damascus (Acts 9). He had heard heavenly words that he could share with no one (2 Corinthians 12:4). Were these the things Paul took greatest delight in? We would certainly rejoice if we had such vital experiences in our ministry for Christ. Instead, Paul found his greatest joy in giving birth to spiritual children. To the Thessalonians he said: "What is our hope, or joy, or crowning of rejoicing?" A "crown of rejoicing" is that which provides the greatest pleasure or joy. "Are not even ye in the presence of our Lord Jesus Christ at his coming? For ye are our glory and joy" (1 Thessalonians 2:19,20).

The Joy of Jesus

In His hour of greatest agony and suffering, Jesus experienced a deep, abiding joy. The writer of Hebrews calls Jesus the author and finisher of our faith who "for the joy that was set before him endured the cross, despising the shame" (Hebrews 12:2). His suffering and death were the travail that birthed men and women into the kingdom of God. This joy was the sustaining strength throughout the ordeal of the cross. As with Jesus and with Paul, the birthing of spiritual children is the greatest joy and delight of the Spirit-filled Christian. This joy can be experienced even in the midst of suffering and tribulation.

A man had a flock of 100 sheep. While counting them at the end of a day of grazing, he found that one was missing. This began a time of trouble and suffering for the shepherd. He imagined the missing sheep cornered by a bear or caught in the underbrush. He was so concerned for the lost one that he left the 99 alone and went after the one. Reason tells

Blessed or happy are the persecuted (the *long-suffering*). Blessed or happy are the merciful (the *kind* and the *gentle*). Blessed or happy are the pure in heart (*goodness*). Blessed or happy are they that mourn and still remain *faithful*. Blessed or happy are the *meek*. Blessed or happy are you when men revile you and say all manner of evil against you falsely—if you exhibit *self-control* and don't strike back.

The reason for the happiness or blessing concludes each beatitude: these on whom God's blessing rests shall be called the children of God, shall see God, shall inherit the earth, shall possess the kingdom of heaven, shall receive mercy and kindness, shall be filled with righteousness, and shall be comforted. As the fruit of the Spirit are produced in our lives, and as we receive God's approval on the Christlike character the Spirit develops in us, a supernatural joy permeates our daily experience.

Finding the Joy of the Lord

Are you joyful in tribulation or suffering? Have others disappointed you through their faithlessness? Do the members of Christ's body seem to be living below the standard God lays down in His Word? Does the power and prevalence of evil seem to defeat the work you desire to do for God? In the midst of these outwardly disheartening circumstances, you can have the supernatural joy of the Lord, the special fruit produced by the faithful Holy Spirit. The joy of the Lord is the strength through which you can conquer Satan's temptation and tribulation. Something glorious is being birthed in your life, if you let the Spirit do His work.

us that he should have found 99 times more joy in what he had left than in what he had lost. But no, he had to go after the lost one. And when the lost sheep was found, he gently lifted it to his shoulder *rejoicing*. Upon arriving home, he called his friends together that they might rejoice with him.

The finding of the one lost sheep brought more joy to the shepherd than did the 99 that needed no individual attention. Joy came after the suffering, because the shepherd loved the sheep that caused him to suffer.

Joy Results From Fruit Bearing

From 1 Corinthians 13 we see that love, the first fruit mentioned in Galatians 5:22,23, includes the other eight. Love finds *joy* in truth. It is not easily provoked; it abides in *peace*. It endures all things with *patience*. Love does not vaunt or assert itself, for it is *gentle* and *kind*. It does not seek its own selfish ends but shows *goodness* to others. In *faith*, love believes all of God's promises and it demonstrates *faithfulness* to God and man as it bears all things. Far from being puffed up, love is *meek* and humble. It never behaves in an unseemly or inappropriate manner; it is in complete *control of self*.

Just as love is found in all fruit bearing, so joy comes as the Spirit-filled Christian manifests the marks of character that Christ wants to produce in our lives. Jesus said it this way: "Blessed are the *peacemakers*" (Matthew 5:9). Blessed . . . happy . . . joyful! Those who demonstrate the fruit of the Spirit and desire to see the fruit multiplied in the lives of others experience the joy of the Lord.

"No chastening [or discipline] for the present seemeth to be joyous, but grievous: nevertheless, afterward it yieldeth the peaceable fruit of righteousness unto them which are exercised thereby" (Hebrews 12:11). Even when the suffering seems to produce anything but joy, the Spirit-filled Christian can have the unspeakable joy of the Lord.

What must the Christian do so the Holy Spirit can produce joy in the midst of suffering? Our carnal nature thinks only of the pain and the suffering. Self-pity intensifies the pain. But we must look beyond the travail to the birth God is effecting. And there are many things we can rejoice in, even during the suffering.

Like David, we can rejoice in our salvation (Psalm 9:14). Knowing that our names are written in heaven is always a source of joy, if we remind ourselves of this precious truth.

We can always rejoice in the greatness of God. He has done great things in the past, and His arm is not shortened today. Some people rejoice in the gifts rather than the Giver. A dearth of expected blessings then brings discouragement and unhappiness. But when our joy is in God, the receiving of gifts has no effect on our joy. To be on the same team with God himself is life's perpetual joy.

There is a song of joy sung by the Christian church around the world. I have heard it in English, in Swahili, and in Luo:

Oh come and go with me to my Father's house,
To my Father's house, to my Father's house;
Oh come and go with me to my Father's house,
Where there's joy, joy, joy.

IV

Peace
and the
Spirit-filled Life

"GLORY TO GOD IN THE HIGHEST, and on earth peace." So sang the herald angels on the night the Prince of Peace was born. But has man so thwarted God's plan in sending Jesus that we have less peace now than the world had a century before the First Advent? Although a cursory evaluation might incline toward such an opinion, we are reminded that God is still sovereign and His ways are certain and trustworthy from beginning to end.

Just as the Father looked on the completed work of His Son at Creation and saw that it was good, so He looked on the finished work of His Son at Calvary, was pleased, and invited Him to sit at His right hand in heaven (Hebrews 1:13).

And when this human manifestation of God himself returned to heaven, having completed His work of redemption, He sent to His followers and their successors the Holy Spirit to convict men of sin and bring them to peace with their Maker. Furthermore, the fruit which the Paraclete produces in the life of the Spirit-filled Christian includes peace: "The fruit of the Spirit is love, joy, peace" (Galatians 5:22).

But man prefers his own way to God's way of peace. He prefers to mouth the word *peace*, use it on his greeting cards, and place its symbol on his automobile bumper, rather than to accept completely God's peace and allow the Spirit of peace to dwell largely in his life. So in today's world the symbols of conflict are much more numerous than the symbols of peace: war casualties, prisoners of war, labor and management disputes, political disagreements, generation gaps and conflicts. And on the international scene, the symbols of conflict are the arms race, the iron and bamboo curtains, and the Berlin Wall. While every mouth speaks peace as a thread of hope for a world of conflict, the symbols of nonpeace flourish.

Peace—the *shalom* of the Old Testament and the *eirene* of the New Testament—has a broad primary meaning of completeness, wholeness, and unity.[1] It was the usual word of greeting or farewell in both Testaments. It is found at the beginning or end of all New Testament epistles except two, James and 1 John. But this broader meaning of the word narrows in the majority of passages to the more commonly accepted meaning of "freedom from strife whether external or internal" or "security from outward enemies as well as calm of heart."[2]

Peace With God

Peace with God is the calm of sins forgiven. And until men make individual peace with God, there is no hope for peace and goodwill among men. Although the benefits of Christ's life, death, and resur-

---

[1] William Gesenius, *A Hebrew and English Lexicon of the Old Testament,* trans. Edward Robinson (Oxford: Clarendon Press, 1952), *s.v.*

William F. Arndt and F. Wilbur Gingrich, *A Greek-English Lexicon of the New Testament* (Chicago: University of Chicago Press, 1957), *s.v.*

[2] E. F. Harrison, ed., *Baker's Dictionary of Theology* (Grand Rapids: Baker Book House, 1960), *s.v.*

rection are manifold, it all began as a means of bringing the creature into peace with his Creator. Man does not make peace with God; he merely accepts the peace God has made through the work of His Son. The initiative was entirely with God. "The chastisement of our peace was upon him" (Isaiah 53:5). The guilty conscience finds peace through the blood of Christ.

Peace With Man

"Blessed are the peacemakers: for they shall be called the children of God" (Matthew 5:9). Christians, of all people, should seek to promote harmony and understanding. The world is full of suspicion, rashness, rivalry, and misunderstanding. But the prayer of the Spirit-filled Christian should be similar to that of Francis Assisi: Where there is suspicion, let me sow trust; where there is rashness, let me sow patience; where there is rivalry, let me sow unity; and where there is misunderstanding, let me be understanding.

It takes more than sheer willpower to be a peacemaker. It demands the fruit of the indwelling Spirit to seek peace with the unlovely and belligerent.

Peacemakers in a world of conflict! But how many Christians find it easier to promote peace among unbelievers than in the body of Christ or the local assembly. If the Spirit dwells in His fullness in two believers, no matter how varied their backgrounds, there should be peace. "For he [Christ] is our peace, who hath made both [Jew and Gentile] one, and hath broken down the middle wall of partition between us" (Ephesians 2:14). Jesus is the peace between ethnic groups, social and cultural classes, educational levels, and age-groups.

But the Scriptures are abundantly clear that peace with his fellowman is not the highest achievement of man. It cannot be peace at any cost—if that cost is compromise with sin.

It was in this context that Jesus said, "Think not that I am come to send peace on earth: I came not to send peace, but a sword" (Matthew 10:34). Christ brings a sword in the struggle with sin, and unless efforts toward peace are accompanied with holiness, they do not have His approval.

"Follow peace with all men, and holiness, without which no man shall see the Lord" (Hebrews 12:14). "Follow righteousness, faith, charity, peace, with them that call on the Lord out of a pure heart" (2 Timothy 2:22). "For the kingdom of God is . . . righteousness, and peace, and joy in the Holy Ghost" (Romans 14:17). James makes it clear that Christians are peacemakers through the proper use of their tongues:

Out of the same mouth come praises and curses. My brothers, this should not be so. . . . Who among you is wise or clever? Let his right conduct give practical proof of it, with the modesty that comes of wisdom. But if you are harboring bitter jealousy and selfish ambition in your hearts, consider whether your claims are not false, and a defiance of the truth. This is not the wisdom that comes from above; it is earth-bound, sensual, demonic. . . . But the wisdom from above is in the first place pure; and then peace-loving, considerate, and open to reason. . . . True justice is the harvest reaped by peacemakers from seeds sown in a spirit of peace (James 3:10-18, *NEB*).

Blessed are the peacemakers who first seek holiness and righteousness.

The Peace of God

The peace of God is "a conception distinctly peculiar to Christianity, the tranquil state of a soul assured of its salvation through Christ, and so fearing nothing from God and content with its earthly lot, of whatsoever sort that is."[3] It has also been defined as "a sense of calm, and a complete absence of hostility and fear in the heart, enabling one to devote his total energies with poise and purpose to the task at hand."[4]

There are many outwardly poised individuals who by sheer willpower seem better able than most to control and conceal their deeper emotions. This, however, is not to be confused with the supernatural fruit of the Spirit which is God-given through the agency of the Holy Spirit. Unfortunately, too many Christians are having to clench their fists and hang on by sheer willpower to achieve even a semblance of the peace they know the child of God should have. The fruit of the Spirit is love, joy, and *peace*—supernatural and profound peace.

The true peace of God is freedom from the nagging, persistent, soul-defying fear of the future. Today's headlines include war, violence, crime, drugs, pollution, and general conflict. Yet the fear of what these may become if they get out of hand is often more crippling to the calm and tranquility of the mind than the actual problem of the moment. But the peace of God, brought through the special work of the Holy Spirit, leaves a serenity beyond understanding instead of the normally expected anxiety.

---

[3] Joseph H. Thayer, *A Greek-English Lexicon of the New Testament* (New York: American Book Company, 1889), *s.v.*

[4] L. Thomas Holdcroft, "Spiritual Fruit: Natural or Supernatural?" *Paraclete*, V (Winter 1971), 24.

Even death—the greatest enemy and the last to be overcome—can strike no chill into the victorious quiet of the Christian when the Holy Spirit is present in His fullness. The testimony of David can be that of every Spirit-filled Christian: "Though I walk through the valley of the shadow of death, I will fear no evil: for thou art with me" (Psalm 23:4). Though the unconverted is terrified by death, the Christian, through the peace of the Spirit, sees it in an en - tirely different light. He can even wait at the hospital for a diagnosis, which people ordinarily dread, and still have peace.

Fear is not dispelled merely by positive thinking or moral courage, but by recognizing the power and sufficiency of God. Such recognition of God's strength is more than lip service; it is faith in that power and an understanding that fear is a sign of unbelief, for it is not of God. "God hath not given us the spirit of fear; but of power, and of love, and of a sound mind" (2 Timothy 1:7).

On four occasions in the Gospels we find Jesus admonishing fearful or anxious listeners, "O ye [thou] of little faith" (Matthew 6:30; 8:26; 14:31; 16:8). Peter certainly experienced physical fear as he began to sink after stepping out of the boat onto the water. But Jesus summed up both the cause and the cure, "O thou of little faith."

On an earlier occasion, the same disciples, in the midst of a violent storm on Galilee with Jesus asleep in the boat, were completely convinced that their boat was going to sink. In fear and desperation they cried out to Jesus; He answered with His rebuke to the disciples followed by His stern rebuke of the winds and the sea.

These moments of fear came at times of crises. But Jesus knew that people who have not a full measure of faith are fearful and anxious even over such commonplace necessities as food, clothing, and shelter. "Wherefore, if God so clothe the grass of the field . . . shall he not much more clothe you, O ye of little faith?" (Matthew 6:30). Peace, the fruit of the Spirit, is available in the day-by-day routine as well as in the crisis. Faith in the power and sufficiency of God, mediated to us by the Holy Spirit dwelling in us, brings the peace of God which is the mark of a sound mind.

But even though Jesus reminded the disciples on several occasions of their lack of faith which produced a painful fear in their hearts, He still found it necessary to speak to them on the subject of peace just before He took His leave of them. But what blessed words! The echo of the shout of the angels at Christ's birth ("and on earth peace") is unmistakable: "Peace I leave with you, my peace I give unto you: . . . Let not your heart be troubled, neither let it be afraid" (John 14:27). Neither let it be timid or shrinking. Why? Because this peace is a special peace: "My peace I give unto you"—the peace that Jesus came to bring as announced by the angels.

Contemplate for a moment the peace of Christ, for this is what the Holy Spirit produces as the blessed fruit of His presence in a life. Jesus displayed remarkable peace as a 12-year-old lad conversing with the most learned men of His day. He revealed absolute peace in the face of rampaging nature on Galilee. His was a majestic calm and serenity before His accusers and persecutors during the agony of Gethsemane, and even while hanging on the cross, for His forgiving spirit could come only from a heart of peace.

His peace is our legacy. He left it to us as a part of His final will before He went away. And the promised Comforter is the bearer of that peace. But like the earlier disciples, we too frequently fail to receive.

Yes, the peace of God means freedom—from fear, from worry, from mental turmoil and pressure, from insecurity and anxiety, from despair and frustration, from spiritual depression, even from discontent.

Paul, through the work of the Spirit as described in Galatians 5:22, 23 could testify, "I have learned, in whatsoever state I am, therewith to be content" (Philippians 4:11). A contented man enjoys the scenery along a detour. And life at times seems so full of detours.

Prescription for Peace

Peace has come to earth in the person of the Prince of Peace. The nations may not receive this peace and its Giver. The unconverted may spurn the free gift. But of all people, God's children who are led by the Spirit should know this supernatural peace.

How does one appropriate the remedy for inner fear, worry, turmoil, and discontent? Although peace is a supernatural work and fruit of the Holy Spirit, there are prescriptions throughout Scripture which the Christian must follow so the Holy Spirit may produce fruit of inner peace.

1. "Casting all your care upon him; for he careth for you" (1 Peter 5:7). "Care," *merimnan,* means anxious care and worry, whereas "careth," *melei,* means concern or tender care. Yes, it matters to Him about you.

2. "Let the peace of God rule in your hearts" (Colossians 3:15). "Rule," *brabeueto,* means to preside or arbitrate (like an umpire). If we would step

aside and let God call the decisions, our worry over the future and an unhealthy fear of missing God's will or guidance would vanish. Many Christians frustrate the gracious purpose of the Spirit, who wants to give them peace, by letting their interests run far afield from those of the Kingdom. "But seek ye first the kingdom of God, and his righteousness; and all these things shall be added unto you" (Matthew 6:33). "These things" includes everything necessary for true peace.

3. Trust in God continually. "Thou wilt keep him in perfect peace, whose mind is stayed on thee: because he trusteth in thee" (Isaiah 26:3). The last phrase is of supreme importance. Mentally imagining a benevolent philanthropist or routinely repeating a name of Deity will not suffice. Complete trust must be present. One cannot trust when he worries; nor can he worry when he is trusting. Perfect peace and calmness come from constant, unbroken fellowship with God.

4. Maintain peace with praise and prayer. "Be careful [anxious] for nothing; but in every thing by prayer and supplication with thanksgiving let your requests be made known unto God. And the peace of God, which passeth all understanding, shall keep your hearts and minds through Christ Jesus" (Philippians 4:6,7).

At times the Spirit-filled Christian is an astonishment to himself. He finds a peace filling his heart and mind when by all ordinary standards he should be tormented with worry and fear. In times such as these, he knows that the Holy Spirit has been faithful in producing the supernatural fruit of heavenly peace —the kind which the herald angels proclaimed and Jesus left in His final will to His children.

V

Patience and the Spirit-filled Life

WE LIVE IN AN AGE very much concerned about individual rights. Certainly the Christian should be concerned about injustices and prejudices as a result of which his fellowman suffers. Unfortunately, this proper concern for the welfare of others is sometimes introverted, and the well-meaning Christian becomes more active in standing up for his own rights. What is justified as "the principle of the thing" is little more than that last temptation to be overcome: human pride.

C. S. Lewis has noted a twofold thrust in the Christian's relationship to his world. "Christianity really does two things about conditions here and now in this world: (1) It tries to make them as good as possible, i.e., to reform them; but also (2) it fortifies you against them in so far as they remain bad."[1]

Some ages have erred in emphasizing the second aspect to the detriment of the first; mysticism and misguided pietism have been the result. Today's age, however, seems more intent on changing the world and has forgotten the inner work of the Spirit which still is extremely important.

---

[1] C. S. Lewis, "Answers to Questions on Christianity," *God in the Dock: Essays on Theology and Ethics* (Grand Rapids: Wm. B. Eerdmans Publishing Co., 1970), p. 49.

Fourth in the list of the fruit of the Spirit (Galatians 5:22), immediately following the familiar triad of love, joy, and peace, is long-suffering or patience. The concept of endurance in the face of hardship, especially when nothing can be done about the suffering, is not new with Christianity. Three hundred years before Christ, a Greek philosopher, Zeno of Citium, advocated a view which has come today to be known as Stoicism. The Stoic philosophers are mentioned once in the New Testament (Acts 17:18): "Then certain philosophers of the Epicureans, and of the Stoics, encountered him [Paul]."

That the Stoic philosophy was still current in Paul's day is also attested by other than Biblical sources. Seneca, the great Roman statesman and philosopher (4 B.C. to A.D. 65), was an almost exact contemporary of the apostle Paul. From Seneca's pen came many essays on the spirit of Stoicism in practical ethics.

Like the pantheists, the Stoics held inanimate objects, plants, animals, man, and even the concept of God to be portions of an overall divine force. That force worked impersonally according to unchangeable laws; it was therefore futile to resist the inevitable. The wise man, fully comprehending this fact, submitted himself to natural law and declared himself free from passion, unmoved by grief or joy, and indifferent to pain or pleasure. Thus the concept of suffering long without resisting was known to these philosophers, but only because they saw no other alternative to hardships. Admirable as their attitude of endurance may have been, it did not grasp anything of the Christian idea of turning suffering into joyful victory over a sinful world.

Old Testament Concept of God's Patience

The Hebrew phrase which is translated "long-suffering" in the Old Testament occurs only four times (Exodus 34:6; Numbers 14:18; Psalm 86:15; Jeremiah 15:15); in each instance it applies to the long-suffering of Jehovah. Three references speak of man's patience, but their meaning seems limited to simple endurance: "Rest in the Lord, and wait patiently for him" (Psalm 37:7); "I waited patiently for the Lord" (40:1); and, "The patient in spirit is better than the proud in spirit" (Ecclesiastes 7:8).

Writers of the New Testament, however, were able to look back on two Old Testament men and see their great patience. "And so, after he [Abraham] had patiently endured, he obtained the promise" (Hebrews 6:15). The Greek word for "patiently endured" is *makrothumeo,* and the corresponding noun is translated "long-suffering" in Galatians 5:22. James reminds his readers of the Old Testament saint who has become the proverbial symbol for patience: "Ye have heard of the patience of Job" (James 5:11). In this instance, however, the more frequently used synonym *hupomone* appears.

Patience or long-suffering is primarily a characteristic of God, in the New Testament as well as in the Old. The purpose of that divine long-suffering is our salvation. "The Lord is not slack concerning his promise, as some men count slackness; but is long-suffering [*makrothumeo*] to us-ward, not willing that any should perish, but that all should come to repentance" (2 Peter 3:9). Later in the same chapter, Peter becomes more specific: "Consider that God's patience [*makrothumia*] is meant to be man's salvation" (2 Peter 3:15, Phillips). Consciousness of the gift of God's patience should inspire the Christian to be long-suffering toward others, in behalf of his Heavenly Father. "Now the God of patience and consolation grant you to be likeminded one toward another according to Christ Jesus" (Romans 15:5).

Patient With Men

There are three Greek words which convey the concept of patience in the New Testament: *makrothumia, hupomone,* and *anoche*. The last of these appears only twice, and both times it refers to the forbearance (holding back) of God concerning man's sinning (Romans 2:4 and 3:25). The remaining two words are so obviously synonyms that some account must be made of their similarities and differences. The fact that Paul on four occasions uses both words in the same list indicates that he then desired to emphasize some fine distinctions. Concerning the differences between these synonyms, Burton L. Goddard observes, "*Hypomone* is the most common NT synonym, pointing to bearing up under suffering or despair, whereas the *makrothymia* word group suggests self-restraint in the face of unsatisfied desire."[2]

Another suggestion is made by an earlier scholar, Richard C. Trench:

Makrothymia will be found to express patience in respect to persons, *hypomone* in respect of things. . . . We should speak, therefore, of the *makrothumia* of David (2 Samuel 16:10-13), the *hypomone* of Job (James 5:11). Thus, while both graces are ascribed to the saints, only *makrothymia* is an attribute of God.[3]

---

[2] *Baker's Dictionary of Theology,* Everett F. Harrison, ed. (Grand Rapids: Baker Book House, 1960), p. 328.

[3] Richard C. Trench, *Synonyms of the New Testament* (Grand Rapids: Wm. B. Eerdmans Publishing Co., 1960 reprint of 1880 ed.), p. 198.

Rather than arrive at mutually exclusive definitions of the two words, we would seem to be safer to recognize these synonyms as functioning much as synonyms function in modern English. When both words are used in the same passage, the fine distinctions are intentionally being emphasized. If only one of the words is used, then both ideas are generally included in the one word.

Thus we can look first at the four Pauline passages in which both *makrothumia* and *hupomone* are used: "[Being] strengthened with all might, according to his glorious power, unto all patience [*hupomone*] and long-suffering [*makrothumia*] with joyfulness" (Colossians 1:11). "But thou hast fully known my [Paul's] doctrine, manner of life, purpose, faith, long-suffering [*makrothumia*], charity, patience [*hupomone*]" (2 Timothy 3:10). And according to the great love chapter, patience is one aspect of love: "Charity suffereth long [*makrothumeo*], and is kind; . . . beareth all things, believeth all things, hopeth all things, endureth [*hupomeno*] all things" (1 Corinthians 13:4,7). Finally, Paul speaks to the Corinthians concerning his credentials as a minister of God: "But in all things approving ourselves as the ministers of God, in much patience [*hupomone*], in afflictions, . . . by pureness, by knowledge, by long-suffering [*makrothumia*], by kindness" (2 Corinthians 6:4,6). Both Goddard's and Trench's definitions shed light on the passages, for suffering, despair, and unsatisfied desire can come into a life either because of persons or because of impersonal trials and hardships. For application to everyday experience, however, the distinction made by Trench is very useful.

One of the most difficult lessons to be learned by the maturing Christian is how to react to unjust treatment at the hands of other human beings, especially other Christians. Obviously, we will not be justly treated simply because we are now children of God. Misunderstanding, misrepresentation, and mistreatment follow the Christian just as they followed Jesus on earth and every other human being. So the question is not whether we will always be rightly treated, but how we will react when we are wrongly treated.

Nor can the Spirit-filled Christian fall into the worldly pattern of "standing up for his rights." True, the world does it, but because of it the world is in chaos. Some human rights are more sacred than life, but they should not be defended in a carnal spirit. And for the individual Christian, God has promised to be the protector: "Beloved, never avenge yourselves, but leave it to the wrath of God; for it is written, 'Vengeance is mine, I will repay, says the Lord'" (Romans 12:19, RSV).

The New Testament passages urging patience in the face of human opposition and misunderstanding are many: "Walk worthy . . . with long-suffering, forbearing one another in love" (Ephesians 4:1,2); "Put on . . . kindness, humbleness of mind, meekness, long-suffering; forbearing one another, and forgiving one another" (Colossians 3:12,13); "Support the weak, be patient toward all men" (1 Thessalonians 5:14); "Take . . . the prophets . . . for an example of suffering, affliction, and of patience" (James 5:10). In each of these instances, some form of *makrothumia* is used.

Patient in Trial and Hardship

Why should anyone need to suffer long? If suffering is necessary, why can it not be brief? There is probably no greater justification for God's allowing suffering than that it produces patience. Some may ask God for the fruit of patience and expect it to be present through an instantaneous gift. But God, through His Holy Spirit, answers the prayer by permitting trials—someone or something to endure—that produce patience. "But we glory in tribulations also; knowing that tribulation worketh patience" (Romans 5:3). "The trying of your faith worketh patience" (James 1:3).

Unfortunately, all suffering does not develop the fruit of patience. If the suffering is a buffeting because of our faults, there is no glory in it, "but if, when ye do well, and suffer for it, ye take it patiently, this is acceptable with God" (1 Peter 2:20). Furthermore, patience in suffering must be linked with faith in God; if it is not, we are mere Stoics. Writing to the Thessalonians, Paul spoke of their "patience and faith in all . . . persecutions and tribulations" (2 Thessalonians 1:4). And the writer of Hebrews urged his readers to be "followers of them who through faith and patience inherit the promises" (Hebrews 6:12).

But why would one desire patience if it requires prior suffering? James gives us one answer: "But let patience have her perfect work, that ye may be perfect and entire, wanting nothing" (James 1:4). Without patience we are incomplete as Spirit-filled Christians. Furthermore, the receiving of God's promises depends on patience: "Patient endurance is what you need if, after doing God's will, you are to receive what he has promised" (Hebrews 10:36, Phillips).

Not only do tribulation and suffering produce patience, but patience, as the fruit of the Spirit, transforms the hardest trial into glory as the Christian sees the purpose of the suffering beyond the present pain. Only then can he face delay without becoming depressed; only then can he endure oppression and suffering without retaliating or relenting. Those servants whom God desires to use in a larger ministry may be confronted by more trials, that after the trials they may be used in greater measure.

The increase of patience, through the working of tribulation, also makes one a good soldier who can endure hardness in the battle against Satan (2 Timothy 2:3). The Spirit-filled Christian is much like the king described by A. E. Housman, who by voluntarily building an immunity to poison was able to overturn later attempts to take his life:

> There was a king reigned in the East:
> There, when kings will sit to feast,
> They get their fill before they think
> With poisoned meat and poisoned drink.
> He gathered all that springs to birth
> From the many-venomed earth;
> First a little, thence to more,
> He sampled all her killing store;
> And easy, smiling, seasoned sound,
> Sat the king when healths went round.
> They put arsenic in his meat
> And stared aghast to watch him eat;
> They poured strychnine in his cup
> And shook to see him drink it up:
> They shook, they stared as white's their shirt.
> Them it was their poison hurt.[4]

[4] A. E. Housman, "Terence, This Is Stupid Stuff," lines 51-74.

Satan seeks to destroy our souls, but through the patience developed as God allows new trials according to our capacity, we can turn Satan's poison back upon himself.

In the natural, suffering tends to produce discouragement and gloominess. But the patience which is produced by the Spirit is accompanied with joyfulness (Colossians 1:11). The true fruit of the Spirit is victorious. It suffers with a smile. To the outsider, there seems to be no trials or suffering. When a long face accompanies suffering, the Spirit is not producing the supernatural fruit of patience.

Patience in Leaders

Gifted people are often known for their impatience with others who are less talented. But the scriptural pattern for leadership in the body of Christ is quite different. Patience is especially commended for Christian ministers and teachers. Paul charged Timothy: "Reprove, rebuke, exhort with all long-suffering and doctrine" (2 Timothy 4:2). Speaking to Timothy of his own experience in patience, Paul said, "I obtained mercy, that in me first Jesus Christ might show forth all long-suffering, for a pattern to them which should hereafter believe on him to life everlasting" (1 Timothy 1:16). Similar encouragements for patience in leaders are found in 2 Corinthians 6:4-6; 2 Timothy 3:10; and Titus 2:2.

How does one measure the degree to which patience has been produced in his life through the ministry of the Holy Spirit? It is easy to think that we are patient simply because we have had no real problems or trials. But the test, the tribulation, both reveals the lack of patience and, if used properly, begins to produce the supernatural fruit of patience. The Spirit-filled Christian behaves with a patience that is beyond the natural. It is more than the passive endurance of the Stoic. It is the active patience which clings steadfastly to God in faith and joyfulness. So let us run with patience—active patience—the race that is set before us (Hebrews 12:1).

VI

Kindness and the Spirit-filled Life

OF THE NINE GREEK WORDS Paul uses for the fruit of the Spirit in Galatians 5:22 and 23, *chrestotes,* rendered "gentleness" by the King James Version, has been the most troublesome for translators. Paul is the only New Testament writer who uses the noun form of the word, although the adjective *chrestos* is also used by Matthew, Luke, and Peter.

Paul uses *chrestotes* 10 times in his epistles, but only in the passage on the fruit of the Spirit does the Authorized Version translate it "gentleness." On the other nine occasions it is translated "kindness" (2 Corinthians 6:6; Ephesians 2:7; Colossians 3:12; Titus 3:4), "goodness" (Romans 2:4; and three times in Romans 11:22), and "good" (3:12).

Yet Paul clearly intended something more specific than "goodness" by his use of *chrestotes* in Galatians 5:22, for the very next word is *agathosune* which in each of its four New Testament appearances is translated "goodness." So a better single-word translation for *chrestotes* as a fruit of the Spirit seems to be "kindness."

This beautiful Greek word is the expression of an equally beautiful grace. The kindness produced as the natural fruit of the Spirit dwelling in His fullness within the Christian, however, needs the full light of

Scripture to give its true meaning. Natural man sees kindness as protecting a weaker person from pain, pressure, and penalty. He will overlook the open sin and lawlessness of a fellow human being, feeling it would be unkind to make an issue over anything that would cause embarrassment or conflict with authority.

But is this true kindness? Goethe, the German poet, called kindness "the golden chain by which society is bound together." In the name of kindness, individuals support causes which claim to restore personal rights to minority and downtrodden groups. These efforts would appear to show the greatest of kindness. Yet our world, our nation, our society seems to be coming apart. The glue of man's kindness does not stick. The world needs Spirit-prompted kindness.

The Pattern for Man's Kindness

The contemporary view of kindness is not that held by God. God is love, and love is kind (1 Corinthians 13:4). Yet God allows man—Christian and non-Christian alike—to experience pain, penalty, and even death. But He shows His kindness *in* these sufferings if He does not remove them. In the midst of sin He shows salvation. His greatest act of kindness was sending His Son so that while in the world, we need not be of that world. His great kindness to Paul was the gift of grace to bear the prick of the thorn in his flesh which was not to be removed (2 Corinthians 12:7). Not only in the ages to come, but even today, God shows "the exceeding riches of his grace in his kindness [chrestotes] toward us, through Christ Jesus" (Ephesians 2:7).

Titus 3:4,5 speaks of "the kindness [chrestotes] and love of God our Saviour" in providing the "washing

52

of regeneration, and renewing of the Holy Ghost." These great gifts make acts of human charity and benevolence seem insignificant. God's kindness, then, is first a concern for our spiritual welfare, and second a concern for our physical well-being as it affects our spiritual condition. Consequently, the greatest kindness we can perform for a fellowman is to bring him to a confrontation with his Creator and Saviour, Jesus Christ. This, however, does not exempt us from showing physical or material kindness to one in need. The Spirit produces the fruit of kindness in behalf of the whole man, both in spirit and body.

The Spirit of Kindness Is Gentle

"Gentleness" as a translation for *chrestotes* is not necessarily a linguistic blunder of 16th- and 17th-century Greek scholars. It simply does not encompass all Paul intended. True kindness is gentle, and the admonitions to Christian gentleness in Scripture are many. "The servant of the Lord must not strive; but be gentle unto all men" (2 Timothy 2:24). "Speak evil of no man . . . but [be] gentle, showing all meekness unto all men" (Titus 3:2). "Let your moderation [literally, *gentleness*] be known unto all men" (Philippians 4:5).

Since it is the Holy Spirit in the believer who produces the fruit, the symbols used in Scripture for the Spirit give a good insight into the fruit which will grow. Thus the dove is appropriately chosen as an emblem of the Spirit of God. In Genesis 1, the Spirit of God moved, brooded, or fluttered upon the dark chaotic waters, dovelike, according to the poet John Milton:

O Spirit . . . thou from the first
Wast present, and with mighty wings outspread,
Dovelike sat'st brooding on the vast abyss,
And mad'st it pregnant.[1]

This gentlest of birds, again representing the Holy Spirit, was present at the baptism of Jesus (Luke 3:22). And when Jesus sent forth His disciples, He commanded them to be "harmless as doves" (Matthew 10:16). The Spirit-filled life will be marked by the dovelike temper and disposition of gentleness.

The Spirit of Kindness Is Tenderhearted

In writing to the Ephesians, Paul gives another admonition to kindness in chapter 4 verse 32: "Be ye kind [chrestos] one to another." But then, as though the exhortation to kindness needed some elaboration, Paul used an adjective and an adjectival phrase to spell out specifically what he meant by kindness to one another. "Be ye kind one to another, [that is] tenderhearted. . . ." This is the aspect of kindness which places the best interpretation on the actions of others and is patient and trusting rather than suspicious, critical, cold, driving, and exacting. This tender kindness of Christ is nowhere better displayed than in the reception of the formerly immoral but now penitent woman at the house of Simon who washed the feet of Jesus with her tears and wiped them with her tresses (Luke 7:37-50).

Compassion for the suffering of another shows a heart of tenderness and kindness. Jesus felt compassion for the neglected multitudes (Matthew 9:36). Miracles of blessing and kindness flowed from this tenderhearted Master. Yet, though He showed such

---

[1] Milton, *Paradise Lost*, Book I, lines 19-22.

great compassion for others, He sought none for himself. Even in the agony of Gethsemane and the pain of Calvary, He was a stranger to self-pity. And as compassion is the antithesis of self-pity, so true kindness is the opposite of self-love and pride. When the Holy Spirit controls the hearts of God's people, the appeal to be kind and compassionate one to another is both natural and practicable.

Kindness is not always an act done to a person in his presence. Probably the greatest unkindnesses are done to people when they are not present. "Behold, how great a matter a little fire kindleth! And the tongue is a fire, a world of iniquity" (James 3:5,6). The tongue can be an instrument of tender kindness or of the greatest unkindness. But the kindness produced by the indwelling Holy Spirit operates whether the object of kindness is present or not.

The Spirit of Kindness Is Forgiving

"Be ye kind one to another, [that is] tenderhearted, forgiving one another, even as God for Christ's sake hath forgiven you." Spirit-prompted kindness is also the disposition to overlook and forgive personal injuries. And in the working out of this fruit of the Spirit lies our own forgiveness and right standing before God. "For if ye forgive men their trespasses, your heavenly Father will also forgive you: but if ye forgive not men their trespasses, neither will your Father forgive your trespasses" (Matthew 6:14,15).

Three of the 10 appearances of *chrestotes* are found in one verse, Romans 11:22. Paul is speaking to Gentile Christians who might be tempted to exult in God's preference for them over the unfaithful Israel who had been cut off. "Behold therefore the goodness [*chrestotes*, kindness] and severity of God: on them which fell, severity; but toward thee, goodness [*chrestotes*, kindness], if thou continue in his goodness [*chrestotes*, kindness]: otherwise thou also shalt be cut off." The kindness of God is His mercy and forgiveness extended to those who have come to believe in Him. Yet we cannot be high-minded (v. 20) about this favor of God. The servant who was forgiven a debt of 10,000 talents but would not show mercy to a debtor of 100 pence lost the cancellation which was given to him. The forgiveness we receive from God must be passed on to those who have committed trespasses against us. "Put on therefore, as the elect of God, holy and beloved, bowels of mercies, kindness [*chrestotes*]" (Colossians 3:12).

The Spirit of Kindness Is Courteous

Courtesy may not be one of the essentials for entrance into the Kingdom, but it is certainly a manifest part of true kindness. The command to "be courteous" (1 Peter 3:8) seems best fulfilled by the presence of the Spirit developing the fruit of kindness, tenderheartedness, forgiveness, and compassion. Courteous language (*chrestologia*, kind words—Romans 16:18) may be used by those who cause divisions in the body of Christ, but the potential abuse of a virtue is no reason for excluding it from the graces developed by the Spirit in the life of a Christian. This courtesy is not learned in the finishing school or the book of etiquette. It is not a veneer which disguises the real self beneath.

So far from being this mere grace of word and countenance, it [*chrestotes*] is one pervading and penetrating the whole nature, mellowing there all which would have been harsh and austere.[2]

Courtesy is kindness in action. Unlike politeness, which may be a mere surface finesse, courtesy is the innate quality of the Spirit-filled soul. To be truly courteous is to be considerate, kind, and agreeable. Courtesy, like its parent kindness, is the oil of smooth human relations.

The Yoke of Christ Is Kind

"Take my yoke upon you, and learn of me; . . . for my yoke is easy [*chrestos,* kind], and my burden is light" (Matthew 11:29,30). The idea that the yoke of Christ is easy may be slightly misleading to some Christians. True, it is easy when compared to the bondage of Satan. But more exactly, it is kind; there is nothing harsh or punitive about it.

The yoke of Christ is kind because the Giver of the yoke is kindness personified. Even the Christians who bore His name in the early centuries became personifications of that kindness through the inner work of the Holy Spirit to the extent that the pagans made derogatory plays on the related words for Christ, Christians, and kindness.

This *chrestotes* was so predominantly the character of Christ's ministry, that it is nothing wonderful to learn from Tertullian (*Apol* 3), how *Christus* became *Chrestus,* and *Christiani* became *Chrestiani* on the lips of the heathen—with that undertone, it is true, of contempt, which the world feels, and soon learns to express in words, for a goodness which to it seems to have only the harmlessness of the dove, and nothing of the wisdom of the serpent.[3]

---

[2] Richard Chenevix Trench, *Synonyms of the New Testament* (Grand Rapids: Wm. B. Eerdmans Publishing Co., 1960 reprint from 1880), p. 233.

[3] Trench, *op. cit.,* p. 235.

Be Ye Kind One to Another

The command to be kind is not merely a general encouragement to treat our fellowman better. The world is in great need of kindness, and a human effort at being kind is far better than no effort at all. But the *chrestotes* of Galatians 5:22 refers to a kindness beyond man's greatest capacity without the work of the Holy Spirit in producing this fruit. It is a kindness which is unconscious and spontaneous. If one has to think about being kind, the effort will fail at the first unguarded moment. When the Spirit dwells within in His fullness, the child of God is moved by an impulsive kindness, just as he formerly responded spontaneously with explosive anger.

The presence of the fruit of kindness in our lives is one of the certain evidences that we are acceptable to God as mediators of His love to others. "But in all things approving ourselves as the ministers of God . . . by pureness, by knowledge, by long-suffering, by kindness *[chrestotes]*, by the Holy Ghost . . ." (2 Corinthians 6:4,6). The absolute necessity that we allow the Holy Spirit to produce in our lives the fruit of kindness is painfully obvious. As Christians the pace of our lives must be decelerated to the extent that fruit can grow. And "the fruit of the Spirit is love, joy, peace, long-suffering, kindness. . . ."

VII

Goodness and the Spirit-filled Life

WHAT IS GOODNESS? Is it simply abstaining from evil? If so, good Christians can be made by rigid restriction and legalism. Is it doing the appropriate thing for a particular time and place? If so, Joseph Fletcher's situation ethics—good is relative to the circumstances—should be advocated.

Or is goodness simply being better than the majority of people who populate contemporary society? In current usage, a man is good if he is loyal to his country, provides for his family, pays his bills promptly, participates in community projects, and keeps his home neat and in good repair. But this looseness of definition has diluted the strength and real meaning of the sixth fruit of the Spirit.

Including goodness in the list of the fruit leads some to regard all Christians as Spirit-filled. The newly converted child of God does display more goodness than he did before his salvation experience. And cannot the same be said for his love, joy, peace, patience, kindness, faith, meekness, and self-control? Good should certainly be found in the lives of all Christians; and even in the life of the professed agnostic or atheist one may find something good. But is this what Paul had in mind when he included goodness in the list of the fruit produced by the Spirit?

The Philosophical Search for Goodness

Ultimate or absolute good was the subject of study and reflection in all philosophical schools of Greece. Socrates held that goodness could be taught. Plato, a student of Socrates, believed that a man could only become good by intellectually comprehending that which is scientifically true. Aristotle, however, separated knowledge and goodness, maintaining that man cannot discover sure and certain principles of goodness but must rely on the opinions of intelligent and wise men to determine the good. There can be no absolute moral standard to govern every action.

This philosophical attempt to attain goodness by knowledge and disputation was prolonged for centuries and occupied the best minds of both Greece and Rome. It has since been debated in the non-Christian cultures and subcultures of both hemispheres. Even as recently as our own century, evolutionists have held that goodness is progressing and that one day man will reach moral perfection, simply through the evolutionary process. But when "God" is removed from the "good," as so frequently happens in secular definitions of goodness, that which is left is nothing (zero).

God's Goodness

Common to each of these attempts to define goodness is the prominence of human effort. But there is a difference between doing some particular act of goodness and being a good man. Someone who is not a good baseball player may now and then make a good play on the field or at bat. But the good player is the one whose muscles, coordination, and stamina have been so trained by innumerable hours of practice that they can now be relied on.

So it is with the fruit of goodness. The training period, however, becomes the work of the Holy Spirit in the life of the Spirit-filled believer. It is the development in the Christian of God's goodness. Five times in Psalm 107 we are exhorted to praise the Lord for His goodness (vv. 1,8,15,21,31). The realities of life, though, sometimes tempt men to doubt the goodness of God in the face of human suffering. But somewhere in God's infinitude is an explanation which will reconcile our dilemma.

If God is wiser than we, His judgment must differ from ours on many things, and not least on good and evil. What seems to us good may therefore not be good in His eyes. . . .[1]

There are aspects of goodness which transcend our ordinary measurements and comprehension.

God, who in His essence is good, is the source of all true goodness. All other beings or things are good only by participation in God's goodness. Or to translate Thomas Aquinas, "Of all things there is one goodness, and yet many goodnesses."[2]

The English language, ironically enough, has nearly a half-score of exclamatory phrases in which the original reference was to the goodness of God: "goodness gracious," "goodness (only) knows," "for goodness' sake," "in the name of goodness," "thank goodness,"

---

[1] C. S. Lewis, *The Problem of Pain* (New York: The Macmillian Co., 1962), p. 37.

[2] *The Summa Theologica*, Question 6, Article 4.

and simply "Goodness!" Other less frequently used exclamations may be found in the 13-volume *Oxford English Dictionary of the English Language* (*s.v.*). If men more seriously called upon the name of God and invoked His goodness in their affairs, they would certainly be more blessed with goodness toward their fellowmen.

Man's Highest Good

Although goodness has its source in God himself, the Bible does speak of good men. Barnabas, in Acts 11:24, is called "a good man, and full of the Holy Ghost." Men may call their peers good according to a variety of standards, but when God describes a man as good, it must be through the imputed goodness of His own Holy Spirit.

Goodness in a man also depends on a proper understanding of his role in God's creation and kingdom. Something is good if it fulfills the purpose for which it was made. After each of the steps of creation, God looked upon what He had made and saw that it was good. At the end of the entire process, "God saw every thing that he had made, and behold, it was very good" (Genesis 1:31). The Fall had not yet disturbed the perfect intent for which it was all created; man still fulfilled his purpose of communion with God. He was still good.

But sin changed that. And now goodness must come through the agent of the Holy Spirit. The fullness of the Spirit should bring the greatest measure of goodness which man can attain.

What is man's highest goodness toward his fellowman? Good is present in a practical interest in man's physical and temporal well-being—social, economic, and medical assistance—but if the recipient is left in spiritual darkness, the benefactor has not touched the greatest good, that of bringing him into God's eternal favor.

Man's goodness, like God's, must be voluntary. It is doing good to others because we want to do them good. This does not mean that we do good only *when* we feel like it; rather, we do good *until* we feel like it. Yet we must recognize that goodness is ultimately a work of the Spirit; each act of goodness issues spontaneously by the generation of God's Spirit.

A holy person is led by the Spirit ... whereby in the lively exercise of grace, he easily distinguishes good and evil, and knows at once, what is a suitable amiable behavior towards God, and towards man . . . and judges what is right, as it were spontaneously, and of himself, without a particular deduction, by any other arguments than the beauty that is seen, and the goodness that is tasted.[3]

The fullness of the Spirit will better guide the Christian in acts of goodness than the strongest reason or rationalization.

Goodness Distinguished From Kindness

One might expect that all the nine facets of the Spirit could have been condensed into the one virtue, goodness. Goodness is divine love in action. It includes the demonstration of patience, meekness, and self-control. The truly good man has joy and peace. But Paul's inclusion of *agathosune* along with the other eight indicates the Holy Spirit wished to convey a specific shade of meaning by inclusion of the word. This is seen further in the fact that *agathosune* fol-

---

[3] Jonathan Edwards, *Religious Affections*, ed. John E. Smith (New Haven: Yale University Press, 1959), p. 282.

lows immediately the word *chrestotes,* a word sometimes viewed as a synonym, but more exactly translated "kindness." The Authorized Version translates
it "gentleness."

Archbishop Trench notes that it is "harder to seize
the central force of *agathosune* than of *chrestotes,* this
difficulty mainly arising from the fact that we have
no helping passages in the classical literature of
Greece."[4] Yet he observes that some commentators
find more activity in *agathosune* than in *chrestotes.*
"*Chrestotes* is potential *agathosune, agathosune* is
energizing *chrestotes.*"[5] Thus the goodness listed by
Paul as one of the fruit of the Spirit is an active goodness, not simply a goodness which accrues through
abstaining from evil.

A zeal for good, for that is what goodness ultimately is, may not always fit our superficial concept
of kindness and meekness. The world expresses contempt for kindness which has no strength to it. Christ
was kind to the hungering sinner, but His zeal for
goodness and truth on one occasion resulted in rebuke, correction, and chastisement. Christ was not
violating the spirit of goodness when He drove the
buyers and sellers out of the temple (Matthew 21)
or when He pronounced such awesome woes against
the scribes and Pharisees (Matthew 23). A zeal for
good may today rise to the point of protest or crusade
against evil.

Of the four times *agathosune* appears in Paul's writings (and in the entire New Testament), two of them
seem to stress this strong ardor for uprightness, "I

[4] Richard Chenevix Trench, *Synonyms of the New Testament* (Grand Rapids: Wm. B. Eerdmans Publishing Co., 1960
reprint from 1880), p. 232.
[5] *Ibid.,* p. 234.

myself also am persuaded . . . that ye also are full of goodness . . . able also to admonish one another (Romans 15:14); "The fruit of the Spirit is in all goodness and righteousness and truth" (Ephesians 5:9).

Active Benevolence and Liberality

Goodness, or zeal for good, must result in positive action as well as protest against evil. There is always a danger of producing a spirituality which is deficient in practical good works. But not so in the Christian whose every act is inspired by the Spirit. "Pure religion [goodness, no less] . . . is this, To visit the fatherless and widows in their affliction, and to keep . . . unspotted from the world" (James 1:27). This is goodness in action. And the more goodness is communicated, the more abundant it grows. We now begin to see the full meaning of goodness: generosity in things material and spiritual. "The liberal soul shall be made fat: and he that watereth shall be watered also himself" (Proverbs 11:25). What we keep for ourselves, we lose. What we give liberally for Christ's sake we keep—in multiplied measure.

Goodness, unlike some of the gifts of the Spirit, is not sensational. If it is done for show, it receives no other reward. Christ cautioned against humanly imitating Spirit-produced goodness. If we do our alms to be seen of men, we have no reward of the Heavenly Father (Matthew 6:1).

Many Christians, unfortunately, seem too busy for plain, simple goodness. Like the priest and the Levite, men of the cloth, they are too engrossed in the trivia of the Kingdom to stop and do the Kingdom work.

Although the text of Luke does not call the Samaritan good, editors have certainly not erred in titling the parable "The Good Samaritan." His business was probably just as pressing, but he was not too busy to stop.

Another form of active goodness is the lost art of hospitality. True hospitality, that is—not social entertainment and exchange of favors. God expects His Spirit-filled children to be "given to hospitality" (Romans 12:13). This outworking of goodness extends beyond the circle of family, friends, and neighbors. When we show goodness without any thought or possibility of repayment, we exhibit true hospitality.

Uneasy consciences can quickly present defenses: "I help anyone I see to be in need, but I don't see many in my daily routine." Goodness, however, is active. It goes out of its way. Jesus did not tell His host in Luke 14 to help the poor, maimed, lame, and blind *who came to his door for assistance*. Rather, He said, "When thou makest a feast, call the poor . . ." (Luke 14:13). Through the impulse of the Spirit, we must seek ways of doing good.

The apostle Paul desired that the Galatians would allow the Spirit to have such control of their lives that supernatural fruit would be produced. There are many human imitations of the fruit, and none is given more lip service than that of goodness. But a great gulf lies between popular goodness as the avoidance of evil conduct and the Spirit-prompted goodness of hospitality, liberality, benevolence, and active protest against evil. God is our goodness; we participate in that goodness through the ministry of His Holy Spirit.

Knowing that God is the source of any goodness which may spring from our lives, we can then give of our whole strength to the growth of that precious fruit.

Do all the good you can,
By all the means you can,
In all the ways you can,
In all the places you can,
At all the times you can,
To all the people you can,
As long as ever you can.

—*John Wesley*

VIII

Faith and the Spirit-filled Life

THE SEVENTH ASPECT of the fruit of the Spirit is a faith-filled life. Stephen was "a man full of faith and of the Holy Ghost" (Acts 6:5). And Barnabas was "a good man, and full of the Holy Ghost and of faith" (Acts 11:24). These men, one a layman and one an apostle, were only two of the many Spirit-filled Christians in the Early Church. Yet Luke's use of the same descriptive terminology confirms that the Holy Spirit is no respecter of persons—or parsons—and that the fruit and the gifts are for all who submit themselves as channels through which the Spirit can flow.

The coexistence of a faith-filled life with a Spirit-filled life is significant, for it underscores the affirmation of Galatians 5:22: "The fruit of the Spirit is . . . *faith*." *Pistis* is the same Greek word which is applied to Stephen and Barnabas.

English Equivalents for Pistis

The majority of 20th-century translations prefer "faithfulness" (Amplified, *The Living Bible*, NEB, RSV, Williams, Wuest) or "fidelity" (Berkeley, Moffatt, Phillips) over the Authorized Version rendering of "faith." It is unfortunate, however, that the choice must be for one to the exclusion of the other. *Pistis*, as distinct from *pistos* (the adjective), appears over

240 times in the Greek New Testament. Over 97 percent of these appearances are rendered "faith" in the King James translation. Other renderings are "assurance," "belief," and "fidelity." Through the use of such synonyms as "trust," "faithfulness," "conviction," "integrity," and "fidelity," the number of times *pistis* is translated "faith" drops slightly to 90 percent in the *New English Bible*. Of the 21 uses of *pistis* in Galatians, however, only in 5:22 does the NEB choose another word, *fidelity*.

It seems obvious, therefore, that *pistis* in Galatians 5:22 is capable of the double meaning of "faith" and "faithfulness." The Christian who is filled and led by the Spirit has an unswerving confidence in God and a humble reliance upon His promises. At the same time, and growing out of his steadfast faith in God, there is a dependability beyond the ordinary. Faith in God produces faithfulness toward God and man.

Growing Faith and Dead Faith

In the life of each believer there is faith. "For by grace are ye saved through faith" (Ephesians 2:8). The Christian stands by faith (Romans 11:20; 2 Corinthians 1:24) and walks by faith (5:7). But experience demonstrates and the Scriptures state that all Christians have not reached the fullness of faith.

In his first epistle to the Thessalonians, Paul expressed concern about a deficient faith in the church: "Night and day praying exceedingly that we might see your face, and might perfect that which is lacking in your faith" (3:10). But by the time he wrote his second epistle to the church at Thessalonica, Paul could compliment them because their faith was increasing mightily (1:3). And each Christian in the congregation at Rome was expected to minister spiritually according to his measure or proportion of faith (Romans 12:3,6).

Since Christ is the author and finisher of our faith (Hebrews 12:2), man can claim no credit for faith; it is the gift of God (Ephesians 2:8). But man can refuse through unfaith or disbelief to let the divine process work. And the task of the Holy Spirit is to produce a full measure of faith as one of the fruit of a Spirit-filled life. Like Stephen and Barnabas, the 20th-century Christian should be full of the Spirit and of faith.

But all faith is not of supernatural origin or consequence. Our society, apart from the strong moral influence of the Church, depends on some degree of faith from each citizen. All interpersonal relationships demand faith in another person for success. Martin Tupper, the 19th-century versifier of homespun philosophy, expressed it well in his *Proverbial Philosophy*:

Never was a marvel done upon the earth,
*   but it had spring of faith:*
Nothing noble, generous, or great,
*   but faith was the root of the achievement;*
Nothing comely, nothing famous, but its praise is
*   faith.*

*   *   *

In faith Columbus found a path
*   across those untried waters;*

*   *   *

Faith in his reason made Socrates sublime,
*   as faith in his science, Galileo;*

71

I set not all in equal spheres:
  I number not the martyr with the patriot;
I class not the hero with his horse,
  because the twain have courage;

    ❀ ❀ ❀

There is a faith towards men,
  and there is a faith towards God;
The latter is the gold and the former is the brass;
  but both are sturdy metal.

Both may be sturdy metal, but only the faith in God can be used to build for eternity. With all its positive aspects, "faith" on the purely human level holds potential danger. James alone, of all the New Testament writers, uses *pistis* to denote bare intellectual assent to truth (James 2:14-26). Unfortunately, this is the faith level of the masses today. Faith without works is only mental acceptance; it is dead (v. 17). The devils also believe that there is one God (v. 19), but mere intellectual assent without subsequent works is lifeless.

This seemingly paradoxical treatment of faith startles the reader who understands from other passages that salvation is by faith alone, and not of works, lest any man should boast (Ephesians 2:8,9). But the apparent conflict melts when one recalls the cultural background against which James was writing. The classical Greek writers used the word *pistis* in their literature to indicate firm belief in anything. For the Stoics, *pistis* had no religious significance; it was merely solidity of character or faithfulness to oneself.[1] Thus James was mimicking the usage of

---

[1] *Theological Dictionary of the New Testament*, Vol. 6, Geoffrey W. Bromiley, trans. Gerhard Friedrich, ed. (Grand Rapids: Wm. B. Eerdmans Publishing Co., 1968), p. 182.

those persons he was seeking to convert. One cannot dispute his major point: a merely intellectual "belief," which the demons also have, will not please God.

This infirm "faith" blinds many today to their need for real faith, an utter trust and dependence on the Father, the Son, and the Holy Spirit. Faith in God demands a great deal more than believing that He exists. People may claim to believe in God, but if they make no attempt to follow Him in obedience, they obviously do not trust Him. This "faith" means nothing. Yet such a "believer" may deceive himself into thinking he has received God's gift of faith simply because he believes in the God of the Hebrews, a historical Jesus, and a Holy Spirit who inhabits man's world. Martin Luther rediscovered justification by real faith. In the preface of his *Epistle to the Romans,* Luther defined faith as "a living, daring confidence in God's grace, so sure that it would die a thousand times for it. Such confidence and such knowledge of God's grace makes a man joyous, gay, bold, and merry toward God and all creatures." The Spirit-filled Christian—not on the basis of a past experience but because of the current glow of an inner presence—is full of this divine work of living faith.

Faith as Act, Fruit, and Gift

Faith as a fruit developed and perfected through a Spirit-filled walk must also be clearly distinguished from the act of faith which brings initial salvation and the gift of faith as a special operation of the Third Person of the Trinity. In all three instances it is the same faith, for the same God gives each. But the act of the human will in accepting the divine offer of grace and in relying completely on Jesus

73

Christ as Saviour is only a beginning. There are lessons to be learned and new dedications to be made; there is growth to be achieved.

Faith again operates as the trusting child of God receives the Holy Spirit in His fullness and bears witness to that new work of grace as the controlling and enduing Spirit gives utterance. But even that experience is not the ultimate demonstration of faith. The fruit must grow until faith permeates every aspect of one's Christian walk with open expressions of commitment, trust, and confidence in the promises and power of God.

Through some Spirit-filled Christian will work, in the Spirit's diversity of operation (1 Corinthians 12:6,9) the special gift of faith, an unusual endowment of faith at a time of special crisis or opportunity. But whether or not this gift operates through a specific Spirit-filled Christian, he still can and should manifest the fruit of living faith as a continuous walk before God.

Faithfulness and the Spirit-filled Life

The Christian full of the Spirit and faith is faithful, for the latter is a natural outgrowth of the life of faith. God is absolutely reliable and constant. In Him is no "variableness, neither shadow of turning" (James 1:17); He is not given to arbitrariness or fickleness; He is unequivocally loyal to His covenants and His promises. His faithfulness cannot be canceled by the faithlessness of man (Romans 3:3; 2 Timothy 2:13).

Man's faith in God grows out of the truth of God's immutability. And the man of faith is himself faithful because he is obedient. Having faith in God involves keeping faith with God. True faith manifests dependability in the discharge of divinely ordained responsibilities, both temporal and spiritual.

Of all the fruit of the Spirit-filled life, the virtue of faithfulness may be the most inconspicuous. The faithful attendant at God's house is taken for granted; constant attention is given to the one who is absent more frequently. When the faithful support the church with tithes and offerings, the church budget is met and everything runs smoothly—often without thanks to the faithful; but the sporadic well-to-do donor is treated with special favor in hopes that he will make a sizable contribution. The pastor who puts his flock first, even rising from a sick bed to perform his duty is seldom appreciated fully; the one who seeks a variety of opportunities and public exposure for himself is constantly told how much he is needed. Though faithfulness is often taken for granted, it is nevertheless one of the most beautiful and necessary of Christian virtues.

John Bunyan knew the importance of faithfulness in the Christian walk and gave it generous treatment on the pages of *Pilgrim's Progress*. Faithful leaves the City of Destruction later than Christian but passes him on the pilgrimage because he never lingers to talk with anyone. He has but one purpose in mind and he faithfully pursues it without wavering. No fellow traveler or chance acquaintance beguiles Faithful from the narrow path. Faithful simply plods on. So does faithfulness.

The faith-filled life is faithful to God; it is also faithful in human relationships. *Pistis,* without question, denotes the reliability of persons, or their faithfulness. The virtue is especially evident in any lasting friendship. Its related attributes are loyalty, honesty, and integrity—faithfulness in word, in deed, and in character. Without faithfulness in human relationships we have fraud, deception, adultery, lawlessness, treachery, cheating, and theft. Any participation in such evil, whether flagrant and open or subtle and hidden, signifies a deficiency in faith and faithfulness.

The servant of God must be a faithful steward (1 Corinthians 4:2). He must be faithful in the small and mundane, for "he that is faithful in that which is least is faithful also in much" (Luke 16:10). A special chapter extolling the faithful heroes of the past would include all the names of Hebrews 11. But it does not take special talent or ability to be faithful. Even the nameless workmen who repaired the temple during the reign of Jehoash "dealt faithfully" (2 Kings 12:15).

The Work of the Spirit

God's ideal of faithfulness cannot be achieved by the natural man, for it is a work of the Spirit. Even the professing Christian church, to say nothing of the unbelieving world, has too few who are what they ought to be in faithfulness. By our original fallen nature, we are unreliable and careless with the truth. We fail both God and man.

But the work of the Holy Spirit is to mold and develop Christlike character. The Christian cooperates in this process by denying himself and allowing the Spirit to produce its own harvest, the wholesome fruit of the Spirit. The life of faith and fidelity is but one of the fruit, but it is a much-needed fruit today. On every hand, even in the church, we see a lack of faith and faithfulness. It may be that we traditional Pentecostals are seeing less fruit of the

Spirit in our lives than some of the unconventional Jesus people and the unorthodox neo-Pentecostals are witnessing in their lives. The Holy Spirit will produce the fruit of faith and faithfulness, but we must allow the river of the Spirit to inundate our lives with the irrigating waters of spiritual vitality.

IX

Meekness
and the
Spirit-filled Life

THE CONTRAST BETWEEN the New Testament and the pre-Christian Greek concepts of virtue is nowhere more observable than in the case of meekness. Nothing in the writings of Aristotle or Plato, or even of the contemporary philosopher and moralist Plutarch, sounds like the meekness seen in Jesus Christ and encouraged by Paul on at least six occasions. According to Archbishop Richard C. Trench, Aristotle saw *praotes* (used for the heathen virtue and later for the Christian grace of meekness) as a state between the two extremes of irascibility and apathy. Plato contrasted the word with fierceness or cruelty. Plutarch thought of it as the opposite of severity.[1]

Praotes, as used by the classical writers, was destined to fall short of the new spirit and meaning given to the word by Christ and His followers, because the two systems were contrary to each other. The mind of the Greek was not the mind of Christ. The pagan Greeks never epitomized meekness or humility as characteristic traits of the ideal Grecian, for they sought only to escape from the world—not to redeem

---

[1] Richard Chenevix Trench, *Synonyms of the New Testament* (Grand Rapids: Wm. B. Eerdmans Publishing Co., 1960 reprint from 1880), p. 151.

it. The noble Greek, as portrayed by Aristotle in *Nichomachean Ethics,* was a dignified and deliberate man. He shunned inferior people and considered meekness an ignoble trait.[2] He was one of the Gentiles to whom Jesus referred in encouraging the disciples to seek to be ministers rather than to be ministered unto: "Ye know that they which are accounted to rule over the Gentiles exercise lordship over them; and their great ones exercise authority upon them" (Mark 10:42).

Christian Meekness Defined

The non-Christian writers of the classical world thought of meekness more as helplessness than as a desirable virtue. Thus, in the Old Testament the virtue of meekness is primarily Godward in its direction. For finite man to display any self-sufficiency before an omnipotent God was pure presumption. Moses, whom Scripture attests to have been the meekest man (Numbers 12:3), seems to have comprehended to an unusual degree the contrast between God's power and his own weakness; this consciousness resulted in great humility and dependence on Jehovah. When weak man appropriated by faith the power of God, he became the instrument for great exploits for Israel.

In the New Testament, however, the word *meekness* acquired the moral significance of humility toward one's fellowman as well as toward God. Thus the Son of Man, the noble example of the New Testament, in contrast to the noble Greek, is seen washing the feet of the disciples in John 13.

---

[2] *Ethica Nichomachea,* trans. W. D. Ross, IV, Chapter 3. The complete text is included in *Introduction to Aristotle,* ed. Richard McKeon (New York: The Modern Library, 1947).

Meekness or humility is the clothing of a servant. It is the opposite of all that is presumptuous, arrogant, forward, and self-asserting. It is freedom from the loathsome disease of pride. It is the expression to men of a spirit that has surrendered voluntarily its claim to independence and has humbled itself "under the mighty hand of God" (1 Peter 5:6). It accepts in exchange for independence a responsibility for taking the good news of redemption to a lost world.

Meekness thus is more than mere gentleness of manner and rests on a deeper foundation than human effort; in its full manifestation it is a fruit of the indwelling and abiding Holy Spirit. A. W. Tozer translates the virtue into practical terms with striking clarity:

The meek man cares not at all who is greater than he, for he has long ago decided that the esteem of the world is not worth the effort. He develops toward himself a kindly sense of humor and learns to say, "Oh, so you have been overlooked? They have placed someone else before you? . . . Only yesterday you were telling God that you were nothing, a mere worm of the dust. Where is your consistency? Come on, humble yourself, and cease to care what men think."[3]

On the other hand, a meek man is not a human mouse with an inferiority complex. He knows that in himself he is nothing; but he knows just as certainly that in God he is everything. The apostle Paul frequently urged the recipients of his epistles to seek meekness. Yet he could also say, "I can do all things through Christ which strengtheneth me" (Philippians 4:13). Meekness does not grow out of

[3] A. W. Tozer, *The Pursuit of God* (Harrisburg, Pennsylvania: Christian Publications, Inc., 1948), pp. 112, 113.

self-abasement but out of an awareness that the mighty hand of God rests over all of life. Moses thus could signal the waters of the Red Sea to part before the Israelites, and Elijah could call on heavenly fire to consume the sacrifice on Mount Carmel, without either forfeiting the inner reality of a meek spirit.

Meekness Toward God

Implicit in a Christian meekness toward God is absolute obedience to the written Word and to the inner prompting of the Holy Spirit. As love slaves of Jesus Christ, all Christians should bend every energy toward pleasing the Master through obedience (1 John 3:22). In meekness, the Christian accepts God's dealings as good, without disputing or resisting. Not only can the meek man sing, "Every promise in the Book is mine," but he *must* also say, "Every chapter, every verse, every line"—including the divine commands, claims, and commissions.

Meekness toward God further involves a teachable spirit. James admonished the Jewish Christians, "Receive with meekness the engrafted word" (James 1:21). Not only is meekness the attitude in which one should receive instruction from God, but it is also the single virtue which Jesus expects the Christian to learn of Him.

The shepherd of a local congregation might wish to learn how to perform miracles in response to Jesus' offer, "Take my yoke upon you, and learn of me." But it is not curing the sick, cleansing the lepers, giving sight to the blind, or raising the dead that we are to learn; these miracles are the work of God himself. Instead, the Christian is to learn to be meek: "Learn of me; for I am meek and lowly in heart" (Matthew 11:29). Such is the excellency of meekness, as if the whole duty of a Christian can be comprehended in that one lesson.

Meekness Toward Men

Although one may find meekness toward God fairly simple to comprehend, the development of meekness toward men is completely beyond the ability of natural man. Wives, in their relationships with their husbands, are to exhibit "a meek and quiet spirit, which is in the sight of God of great price" (1 Peter 3:4). Christian leaders do well to exhibit meekness toward their subordinates rather than judgment and vindictiveness. Paul, writing to the wayward Corinthians, asked the rhetorical question: "What will ye? shall I come unto you with a rod, or in love, and in the spirit of meekness?" (1 Corinthians 4:21). Meekness even enters into one's attitude toward a Christian brother who has offended and needs forgiveness: "If a man be overtaken in a fault, ye which are spiritual, restore such a one in the spirit of meekness" (Galatians 6:1).

But the greatest test of meekness comes in our contact with those who oppose us—and particularly with evil men. On one occasion David was openly cursed and abused by Shimei (2 Samuel 16:5-13). When asked by Abishai, however, for permission to go over and "take off his head," David who had already learned meekness before God replied, "My son, which came forth of my bowels, seeketh my life: how much more now may this Benjamite do it? let him alone, and let him curse; for the Lord hath bidden him. It may be that the Lord will look on mine affliction, and that the Lord will requite me good for his cursing this day" (vv. 11,12).

At another time, again in the midst of trouble, the meek spirit of this great king revealed inner strength and greatness: "They also that seek after my life lay snares for me: and they that seek my hurt speak mischievous things, and imagine deceits all the day long. But I, as a deaf man, heard not; and I was as a dumb man that openeth not his mouth. . . . For in thee, O Lord, do I hope: thou wilt hear, O Lord my God" (Psalm 38:12,13,15). David's faith in God—a faith so strong that David was not afraid to show a meek spirit even before his enemies—was amply rewarded. A meek man is not meek because of what he expects to gain by it, but he gains nevertheless.

The spiritually weak, lacking the fullness of the Spirit within, seek to defend themselves; but self-defense is not meekness. Whereas the self-centered man must constantly build and defend his ego, the yielded, Spirit-filled Christian need not defend himself. God is his defense. God himself intervenes in the affairs of men on behalf of a truly meek man.

Moses, the meekest of all men, was the God-appointed leader of the Israelites. Yet Miriam and Aaron felt that he assumed too much authority when he claimed to speak for Jehovah (Numbers 12:1-15). But rather than defend his God-given prerogatives, Moses meekly placed the whole matter before God. The leprous condition of Miriam was a more eloquent defense than Moses could ever have composed. And when other Hebrews challenged Moses' authority, God's judgment fell on Korah, Dathan, and Abiram as the earth opened and swallowed them alive. Then fire from heaven consumed 250 men who also opposed the meek servant of Jehovah (Numbers 16).

Paul's admonition to Titus to teach the Cretan

84

Christians to show "all meekness unto all men" (Titus 3:2) sums up the matter. Whether a Christian wife before her husband, a Christian leader before his followers, a mature Christian toward an offending or stumbling brother, or a Christian before sinners and evildoers, the Spirit-filled child of God will exhibit the fruit of meekness. "Blessed are the meek."

The Meekness of Christ

The paradoxical combination of meekness and greatness is well illustrated in the life of Jesus. As a fulfillment of prophecy at the Triumphal Entry, the proclamation was made: "Behold, thy King cometh unto thee, meek, and sitting upon an ass, and a colt the foal of an ass" (Matthew 21:5). The King comes! And the one adjective used to describe Him emphasizes His meekness—not His majesty, glory, or power, but His meekness. The trial and crucifixion of this King also fulfilled the prophecy concerning the spirit of meekness in which the Messiah was to come: "He was oppressed, and he was afflicted, yet he opened not his mouth: he is brought as a lamb to the slaughter, and as a sheep before his shearers is dumb, so he openeth not his mouth" (Isaiah 53:7).

"Let this mind be in you, which was also in Christ Jesus" (Philippians 2:5). But how is this likeness to Christ to be acquired? Only by conversation and communion with Him through the indwelling fullness of the Holy Spirit. This Third Person of the Trinity, sent by Christ himself, testifies of the Son (John 15:26) and produces the fruit of meekness in the life of the Spirit-filled Christian.

The meek are mighty in God's eternal plan and purpose. In fact, one of the key truths of Christ's teaching is that the kingdom of God—all the wealth and blessing of heaven—is reserved especially for the meek and humble. "Blessed are the meek: for they shall inherit the earth" (Matthew 5:5), "and shall delight themselves in the abundance of peace" (Psalm 37:11). Paul's call to Timothy still challenges each Christian to produce the fruit of meekness through the help of the Holy Spirit: "O man of God, flee these things; and follow after . . . meekness" (1 Timothy 6:11).

X

Temperance and the Spirit-filled Life

LAST ON THE LIST OF THE FRUIT OF THE SPIRIT is temperance or self-control. Its place in the order does not indicate unimportance, but rather that it regulates all the other fruit or virtues of the Spirit. Love without restraint becomes passion; joy without moderation becomes frivolity; peace without temperance becomes idleness; patience without balance is apathy; gentleness without temperance is weakness; goodness without control becomes fawning; faith without moderation of reason becomes blind superstition; and meekness without temperance is timidity.

Temperance, or moderation through self-control, applies only in the area of the legitimate. For the Christian there is no such thing as temperance in wrongdoing. Any participation in the works of the flesh—unfaithfulness, uncleanness, hatred, wrath, strife, envy, and the other evils mentioned in Galatians 5:19-21—is a warring against the Spirit who is the source of our salvation. Temperance, therefore, is the fruit of a Spirit-filled life which enables one to control his natural desires and inclinations in the interest of higher ends and ideals.

The Greek word translated *temperance* in Galatians 5:23 is *egkrates*. At the time of the King James translation, *temperance* was an accurate translation, for it then meant "self-control." One other Greek word, *sophron*, is also translated *temperance,* and it has the closely related meaning of "sound or soberminded" (Titus 2:2). Thus it is plainly evident that the New Testament virtue or fruit of the Spirit, temperance, refers to an inward power of self-control and moderation, or a freedom from extremes.

A Pagan Concept of Self-control

Unlike some of the other virtues which the New Testament uniquely stresses, self-control is a foundational virtue in many non-Christian ethical systems. Without a personal God-man relationship, such codes must bring to bear some resident power in man to control an otherwise rampant animalistic behavior. This, of course, is man's reason. Aristotle, in *Nicomachean Ethics,* saw temperance as a balance between man's reason and his passion:

The appetitive element in a temperate man should harmonize with the rational principle; for the noble is the mark at which both aim, and the temperate man craves for the things he ought, as he ought, and when he ought; and this is what rational principle directs.[1]

Aristotle thus viewed temperance as the fundamental virtue. Since lack of self-control reduces man to the level of animals, Aristotle felt temperance was the first step to becoming a man in the true sense of the word. He further warned that natural appetites had to be brought under the control of reason at an early age if a child was to become a mature adult.[2]

[1] *Ethica Nichomachea,* trans. by W. D. Ross, Book III, Chapter 12. The complete text is included in *Introduction to Aristotle,* ed. Richard McKeon (New York: The Modern Library, 1947), p. 373.
[2] *Ibid.*

Aristotle's portrait of the temperate man is admirable for an ethical system which relies wholly on the human strength of man:

He neither enjoys the things that the self-indulgent man enjoys most—but rather dislikes them—nor in general the things that he should not, nor anything of this sort to excess, nor does he feel pain or craving when they are absent, or does so only to a moderate degree, and not more than he should, nor when he should not, and so on; but the things that, being pleasant, make for health or for good condition, he will desire moderately and as he should, and also other pleasant things if they are not hindrances to these ends, or contrary to what is noble, or beyond his means. For he who neglects these conditions loves such pleasure more than they are worth, but the temperate man is not that sort of person, but the sort of person that the right rule prescribes.[3]

The description seems to fit the strength Aristotle saw in man. But there should be a marked difference between the self-control seen in the life of a child of God and that seen in the life of a well-ordered and humanly self-disciplined worldling. The Holy Spirit provides a resource beyond the natural strength of man.

Need for Self-control

Self-control is not a luxury to be added to other Christian virtues if one finds it convenient to do so. Rather, it is one of the identifying signs of the Spirit-filled Christian. It is the third of seven virtues Peter claims should, with all diligence, be added to faith (2 Peter 1:5-7). It is one of the virtues which assures the Christian of being "neither . . . barren nor un-

---

[3] *Ibid.*, p. 372.

fruitful" and of making his "calling and election sure" (vv. 8,10). Without it, a person is nearsighted, even blind, concerning spiritual matters (v. 9).

Temperance or self-control is an essential quality of good leadership both in the Church and in the world. Not only should leaders be examples of self-control, but they should also encourage youth in the learning and practice of self-control.

Paul's epistle to Titus, written against a background of an intemperate Cretan society, especially stresses this. Titus was instructed to appoint elders or bishops in every town (1:5); each one as a church leader was to be, among other things, "master of himself" (Moffatt) and "self-controlled" (1:8, NAS). Later in the same letter, Paul tells Titus that the older men should be temperate (2:2). On the other hand, the young women had to be taught by the older women to be "discreet" (2:5) or "temperate" (NEB). Titus was to exhort the young men to be "sober-minded" (2:6) or "temperate in all things" (NEB).

The tenor of the passage is clear. Leaders and older Christians were expected to have learned the virtue of temperance through the life of the Spirit; the younger men and women were to be assisted in every way possible to come to the same life of temperance as quickly as possible.

The implications for the present age are evident. This is the age of youth. By sheer weight of numbers, the voice of the age-group under 20 is demanding to be heard. Yet by the very nature of youth, the virtue of temperance is scarcely beginning to develop, either through natural experience or through the work of the Spirit. The college campus, the metropolitan ghetto, and the political or public meeting are all resounding with the dissent and intemperance of youth. The prophetic voice is needed today more than ever before to broadcast the Biblical injunction to self-control.

Areas of Self-control

Some Christians reflect the opinion that just as patience operates in the face of adversity or affliction, so self-control or moderation operates only in the realm of our pleasures and prosperity. But even one's response to calamity or bereavement must be tempered by self-control. In general, however, self-control as a fruit of the Spirit should operate in three areas of a Christian's life: his use of the provisions of God's nature, his use of man-made pleasure, and his response to inner emotions and passions.

The most wholesome and delicious food and drink may turn to surfeit by excess of eating or drinking. How many persons very properly advocate abstinence from some indulgences which are harmful to body and mind, yet through immoderation in the use of legitimate foods bring harm to their own bodies. In this day of leisure time, sports and recreation are becoming increasingly popular. But if they take up all of a man's time, his life is unprofitable; instead of renewing his strength, they can consume it.

Man-made pleasure can appeal to the senses or the intellect. Moderation or modesty in dress is a specific command of Scripture (1 Timothy 2:9). Man's enjoyment and creation of art, music, and literature must be tempered with self-control. Only eternity will reveal how many Christians have been drawn from a complete submission to God's will by overindulgence in some legitimate pursuits. The answer is not a blanket disavowal of these man-made pleasures as some have advocated, but a self-control in their use which makes them subservient to higher purposes.

Closely allied with the word *temperance,* especially in etymology, is the word *temperament.* The psychology of the inner man—his emotions and passions—is indeed complex; yet man cannot excuse his behavior by simply saying, "That's my temperament" or "That's the way I'm made." Bitterness, anxiety, anger, inordinate love, violent striving for position, apathy, resentment—these are but a few of the defects to which natural man is heir. Without the tempering influence of the Holy Spirit in man's inner emotions and passions, the crowning piece of God's creation identifies more closely with the animal world than with the divine world from which he came.

Unfortunately, man too frequently seeks to justify his intemperate behavior by attributing it to an animal nature over which he has no control and for which he has no responsibility or accountability. But in doing so, he is living far below God's intent for him, and the accountability is in no way diminished. God provides the power through the Holy Spirit; man is responsible for drawing on this resource.

Place of the Spirit in Self-control

It is indeed significant that self-control is one aspect of the fruit of the Spirit. Self is unable to control itself; thus no human effort can achieve the consistent self-control which is demanded by the New Testament ethic. But the Holy Spirit shows self its inadequacies, forcing it to rely on the power of God to develop the fruit of self-control.

Man in his own strength usually can avoid the extreme of murder; but it takes a supernaturally strengthened inner power to avoid the anger which may motivate the murder. The Law put penalties on the worst passions and violence of a fallen nature, but the Holy Spirit fills the life and brings self-control even into the areas of motives and unconscious desires. Man can tame or control animals, birds, and sea creatures, "but the tongue can no man tame" (James 3:7,8). Only the Holy Spirit dwelling within can control this most unruly of members. The fact that a Christian speaks with supernaturally prompted utterance at the initial infilling of the Spirit is one of the most eloquent reminders that the Holy Spirit is the indispensable factor in the control of one's being. The Spirit-filled life which follows should be distinctly marked by a degree of temperance uncommon to natural man.

The Power of Self-control

The preaching of self-control brings conviction on the intemperate hearer. Felix trembled as Paul reasoned with him of righteousness, temperance (self-control), and judgment to come (Acts 24:25). As a standard which man cannot attain in his own strength is held before him, his need for dependence on a higher Power becomes more painful.

Mastery of self was a most notable trait in the lives of the great men of the Bible before they performed the dynamic and miraculous feats for which they are most remembered. Moses learned to discipline self in the backside of the desert before he was entrusted with the leadership of Israel. The disciples learned the rigors of self-control and received the enduement and discipline of the Spirit before they became the pillars of the Early Church. Paul grappled with self in the isolation of Arabia before he became the dynamic apostle to the Gentiles. Self-control through Spirit-control precedes the full manifestation of the power of God.

Self-control also makes a Christian a better servant of Christ. The frequent identification of the writer of a New Testament epistle as a servant or bondslave of Jesus Christ (Paul to the Philippians and to Titus; James, Peter, and Jude in introducing their epistles) was not a mere formality. These were servants of Christ in every sense of the word; self was completely under control. And the witness of these servants through oral and printed word was the most effective Christianity has known from that day to this.

The Reward of Self-control

Self-control is not easy. It is torture to the old man. But Paul, familiar with the athlete's willingness to endure the pains of body conditioning for the passing honor of receiving a soon-to-fade laurel wreath, speaks of the much higher reward that comes to the Christian who has learned self-control. "Now every athlete who goes into training conducts himself temperately and restricts himself in all things. They do it to win a wreath that will soon wither, but we [do it to receive a crown of eternal blessedness] that cannot wither" (1 Corinthians 9:25, Amplified). Peter, too, spoke of receiving "a crown of glory that fadeth not away" when the chief Shepherd shall appear (1 Peter 5:4). But the greatest reward for the Christian will be to live eternally in the presence of the Spirit he has come to know so well in learning the lessons of self-control throughout this earthly existence.